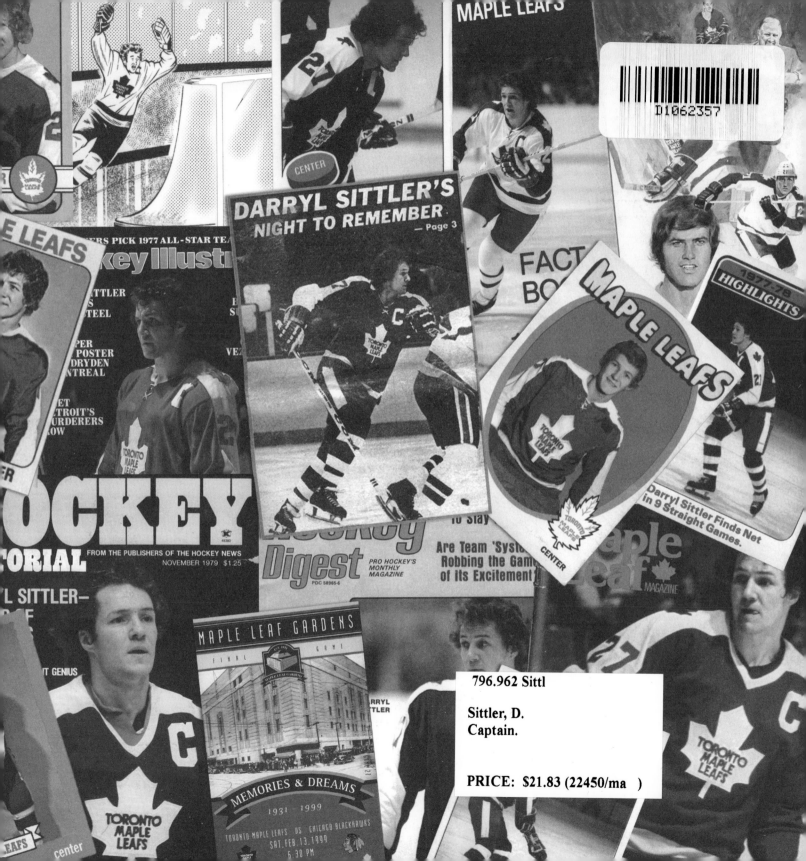

DARRYL SITTLER

WITH MIKE LEONETTI

CAPTAIN

MY LIFE AND CAREER

McCLELLAND & STEWART

TO WENDY AND LUBA

Library and Archives Canada Cataloguing in Publication

Sittler, Darryl, 1950–, author
        Captain / Darryl Sittler and Mike Leonetti.

Issued in print and electronic formats.
ISBN 978-0-7710-7273-4 (hardback).—ISBN 978-0-7710-7274-1 (epub)

        1. Sittler, Darryl, 1950–. 2. Hockey players—Canada—Biography.
I. Leonetti, Mike, 1958–, author II. Title.

GV848.5.S57A3 2016   796.962092   C2016-901361-8
                                                 C2016-901362-6

Jacket image: Portnoy/Hockey Hall of Fame; spine: Hockey Hall of Fame;
back: Harold Barkley; flap: Toronto Star
Front case (courtesy of author); back case (Toronto Star);
ticket stub in endpapers (Hockey Hall of Fame)

Book design: Andrew Roberts

Printed and bound in China

McClelland & Stewart,
a division of Penguin Random House Canada Limited,
a Penguin Random House Company

www.penguinrandomhouse.ca

1 2 3 4 5 20 19 18 17 16

 Penguin
Random
House

CONTENTS

VI   FOREWORD BY JOHN IABONI

IX   INTRODUCTION BY MIKE LEONETTI

XII   ONE: 1976: A MAGICAL YEAR

20   TWO: FROM ST. JACOBS TO LONDON

36   THREE: THE ROOKIE

70   FOUR: THE CAPTAIN LEADS

100   FIVE: GREAT OPPONENTS

120   SIX: MY LAST DAYS AS A MAPLE LEAF

154   SEVEN: HONOURS

178   EIGHT: MY FAMILY

208   DARRYL TODAY: Q&A

210   FOR THE RECORD

212   ACKNOWLEDGEMENTS

FOREWORD

BY JOHN IABONI

Stunning . . . unprecedented . . . daring . . . zany . . . emotional . . . recorded for all time.

Those words applied to Darryl Sittler when he became the first – and of this writing, still the only – player in NHL history to record 10 points in one game. In my view, they also relate to those of us in the media who watched the achievement unfold. When the cheers subsided we were the sole sources to relive it, encapsulate it, and bring our followers behind the scenes.

These were the days of 8 p.m. game start times, with this monumental contest ending at 10:27 p.m. – the "27" extremely fitting for the star of the night. Our approach was to do "running" copy after each period and top the story with a quick lead for our first edition, which had to be on press by 11 p.m. Our later edition would clear at midnight, allowing a little extra time for a rewrite.

Now remember that we had no email, cellphones, Twitter, Instagram. A telecopier operator would put each typescript page on the fax machine drum for the six-minute transmission via telephone back to another machine at our office at 333 King Street East. That was about as "instant" as we knew back in the day.

The first period showed a promising night for Sittler (two assists) and the Maple Leafs (up 2–1) but nothing like what was about to unfold. Over the next 20 minutes, Sittler had electrified everyone with a hat trick and two more assists. That had me constantly turning to our only source of reference in those days – the 1975–76 NHL Media Guide with All-Star Game photos of Ken Dryden and Eddie Westfall on the cover.

Page 121: Chicago's Les Cunningham (January 28, 1940, against Montreal) and Max Bentley (January 28, 1943 against New York) along with Boston's Leo Labine (November 28, 1954) each had the NHL record with five points in one period. Sittler had just joined them.

Page 118: Montreal's Rocket Richard (December 28, 1944, against Detroit) and Bert Olmstead (January 9, 1954, against Chicago) headed the list for most points in one NHL game with eight.

Could/would Sittler tie them? Could/would he get nine? What about ten? Nah! Hey, why not?

That carom shot off Brad Park to catapult Sittler into double-digit territory truly capped the surreal night. So I hurried like someone possessed, pounding those typewriter keys into submission. I ran down to get a quick quote from Harold Ballard (in which he said Sittler's feat was even greater than Paul Henderson's Game 8 goal in the 1972 Summit Series against the Soviet Union and promised to reward his captain with some kind of heirloom). I went to a payphone to dictate that quote to a copy editor for insert into the main game story for that first edition.

Then I headed to the dressing rooms for quotes to cover sidebar/colour stories. En route I ran into Wendy Sittler, whose glowing smile was a story unto itself. She was so proud of her husband – and elated that Sittler's parents, Ken and Doris, were able to attend the game. The next day, Sittler told me that his parents got tickets to the game at the last minute because Greg Hubick's wife wouldn't be using them. Talk about something being meant to be!

Once I got to Sittler in the dressing room, there he was sipping on champagne. Only days before, while Darryl was mired in a scoring slump, Ballard lamented to the media that he needed a centre for his club.

"Mr. Ballard still looking for the centreman, eh?" Sittler said, grinning from ear to ear.

"It was one of those nights when everything happened," he said. "Some nights you have the puck and nothing happens. It'll be hard to forget something like this."

Citing that his pregame ritual was nothing different, Sittler did add, "Well, my son (Ryan) fell in the mud when I was babysitting him ... other than that, nothing different."

Leafs coach Red Kelly commented that Sittler's night was a "fantastic performance which couldn't have happened to a greater guy." Bruins coach Don Cherry added, "Everything Sittler touched turned to gold tonight but he sure worked for them. He's just a great centre."

Coincidentally, Sittler and Cherry collaborated for Team Canada some seven months later, when the Leafs captain capped his remarkable 1976 with the Canada Cup–winning goal against Czechoslovakia.

In between, Sittler thrilled fans once more with his five-goal playoff game on April 22, 1976, in that seven-game war against the Philadelphia Flyers. Covering the Leafs during the Sittler years produced numerous exceptional moments complete with highs and lows.

He was the leader of a franchise that boasted world-class talents such as Borje Salming and Lanny McDonald. It was a squad that was inspired by Sittler's determination but fell short in the depth that the championship teams of that time – the Flyers, Canadiens, and Islanders – possessed. This was a time when we, as beat reporters, travelled on the same buses and charters as the Leafs and stayed at the same hotels. We knew each other by name, which was both good and tense at times. It wasn't unusual over the course of each long season for players and management to confront us over what we'd written about them. Words would be exchanged and then we'd get on with it.

Sittler, as captain, accepted the responsibility it brought and was never afraid to speak his mind. In the end, his departure from Toronto was a devastating loss on all counts, considering I always believed he should have ended his career as a Leaf. His return to the fold when Cliff Fletcher came on board in 1991 was classy and the right thing for the organization to do.

I consider myself fortunate to have been there to document most of Sittler's accomplishments with the Leafs. His ten-point night was unbelievable for him and a career highlight for me as well.

John Iaboni covered the Toronto Maple Leafs for The Toronto Sun *from 1971 to 1984 and was executive editor/writer for the Leafs'* Game Day Program *from 1991 to 2015. In 2010 he became the sixth person – and third writer – to be added to the Media Wall of Honour in the Foster Hewitt Media Gondola at the Air Canada Centre.*

INTRODUCTION
BY MIKE LEONETTI

By the middle of the 1970s, the Toronto Maple Leafs had some of the best players in hockey on their team.

They had exciting players like Ian Turnbull, Errol Thompson, and of course, the tough but talented Dave "Tiger" Williams. In 1976–77 they added the acrobatic Mike Palmateer in net, and he would become one of the most popular Toronto goalies of all time. They had Hall of Famers Lanny McDonald and Borje Salming and captain Darryl Sittler – my new Maple Leaf hero. While there would be no championship, it was still an exciting time to be a fan of the Maple Leafs.

The 1975–76 season started out with Darryl Sittler being named team captain, replacing Dave Keon in that role. At some point that year, the Maple Leafs put all remaining regular-season games tickets on sale at 11 a.m. on a Saturday morning at the Gardens. I lined up with a friend of mine around nine o'clock and sometime around 12:30 or 1:00 we finally got to the ticket window. After inquiring about what was left, we were told there were seats available for the Maple Leafs/Bruins game to be played on Saturday, February 7, 1976.

"Let's get that game. The Bruins are a good team," my friend wisely advised, but I stopped to think for a minute. The Maple Leafs had a home game on Sunday, February 8, against Minnesota. "Listen, why don't we get the Minnesota game and watch the Boston game on *Hockey Night in Canada*? This way we can see both games over the weekend." It should be noted here that the Maple Leafs rarely played at home on a Sunday in those days and there was not going to be any television broadcast of the Leafs/North Stars game – it would only be available on radio. I wish my buddy Joe would have put up a harder fight for the Boston game but he sort of shrugged and said OK.

I could never have anticipated that my hero would have the greatest night in hockey history against Boston, but that is exactly what happened when Sittler recorded six goals and four assists on February 7. Yes, I watched it on TV and all the time the Sittler show was going on, I kept thinking to myself, "I could have been there!" The next night the game against Minnesota was one of the worst ever played in the history of the Gardens. The only good thing was that the Maple Leafs won 4–1 to sweep the weekend at home, but it was a dull, boring contest and I was actually glad when it was over. The lesson to be learned is to always go with your instinct, and taking in a Saturday night game against an "Original Six" team at the Gardens would have been the right thing to do. But that is the kind of Toronto hockey fan I was, so I missed out on some great hockey history just so that I could watch *another* Maple Leafs game!

Darryl Sittler's performance that night was truly remarkable but it was not the first time he had made an impression on me. I recall his rookie season in 1970–71, when this big kid joined the Maple Leafs as a 20-year-old. I can still recall his first career goal against Detroit, and it came after he had an interview with *HNIC* host Ward Cornell, which was a rite of passage in those days. By his third NHL season Sittler had become the Maple Leafs' leading scorer and was clearly on his way to a great career in the NHL.

By the middle of the 1980s I had started to write hockey books, and sometime in the late 1990s I decided to write a children's book about a kid who wanted the sweater of his Maple Leafs hero. The Montreal Canadiens had such a story out about Maurice "Rocket" Richard and I thought Maple Leaf fans deserved one too. After having a debate about which Maple Leaf to focus on, it became clear that Darryl Sittler was the best choice.

The story centred on his 10-point night versus Boston, and even though I have done many other kids' stories involving other hockey heroes – like Bobby Orr, Wayne Gretzky, Mario Lemieux, Wendel Clark, and Sidney Crosby, among others – it is the Sittler-based *My Leafs Sweater* (first published in 1998) that remains the best seller. I know that Darryl is pleased that he has a kids' book out there about his magical night, and many who have read it tell him he is their hockey hero even though they have never seen him play!

In the summer of 2015 I was able to speak to Darryl once more, and we decided that we would work together again. Darryl had already published two fine books, but we have updated many events in Darryl's life and surrounded them with a great number of interesting photographs. It was a great honour for me to do this book, and I was able to interview Darryl a number of times at his home. Darryl shared many memories, not only about the Maple Leafs and hockey, but also about the events that have helped shape his life.

Ian Turnbull, Borje Salming, Errol Thompson, and Lanny McDonald ▶
help celebrate one of Darryl Sittler's ten points against Boston.

It has been said that getting too close to your heroes can be a bit of a dangerous thing. How can anyone live up to the expectations and perceptions that were developed at a distance? It turned out I had nothing to worry about. I think Darryl Sittler is more of a hero to me now than when he played for the Maple Leafs, and I thought that would be hard to do! One major reason for that is Darryl's dedication to so many great causes and charities – it is truly amazing and inspiring. He shows no sign of slowing down when it comes to helping out with worthy events. I quickly found out his calendar is always full!

If I had to summarize Darryl Sittler's life, I would say that he has lived the all-Canadian dream of a small-town kid who wants to make it to the NHL. He certainly accomplished that, and he did it in very impressive fashion under the bright lights of a big city like Toronto, where hockey matters. It was a terrific experience for me to reflect on Darryl's journey. I hope you will enjoy the text and photos as much as I did putting it all together.

Thanks, Darryl!

ONE

1976: A MAGICAL YEAR

There was nothing unusual happening on the morning of Saturday, February 7, 1976. We held the normal pre-game skate at Maple Leaf Gardens and then went home before returning around 5:30 to prepare for the eight o'clock contest. Since the game was going to be on *Hockey Night in Canada*, and the Leafs were facing an Original Six team in the Boston Bruins, there were more media and more people around than usual, but we were used to that being the case when one of the best teams in the National Hockey League came in for a visit. The Bruins, coached by Don Cherry, were coming in on a great roll. They'd won 14 games since December 26, losing just one and ending another in a tie. They'd just won seven in a row to bring their record to 32–10–9 (they would go on to win a total of 48 games in 1975–76 on their way to recording 113 points). The Maple Leafs were 21–20–11.

A day or two earlier, Toronto owner Harold Ballard had sounded off in the newspapers about how top wingers Lanny McDonald and Errol Thompson could really use a top centre for their line since the guy playing there now – Darryl Sittler – was proving to be inadequate! It was pure Harold; he loved getting the headlines. I certainly didn't welcome this type of publicity, but it was something I was used to at this point in my career with the Maple Leafs, despite being named captain in July 1975. Maybe Harold didn't like that, on the day I got the captaincy, I told him he treated some great players, like Dave Keon and Norm Ullman, pretty badly. They had done so much for the team and should have been treated respectfully, which is why I brought it up. But you never knew when Ballard would react or how he would do it.

There was no team meeting that morning – no review or scouting report of the Boston roster and nothing about what game strategy we were going to implement. We just did our normal skate and some drills. We were aware that goaltender Gerry Cheevers was returning to the Bruins from the World Hockey Association but had no idea if he would be playing that night. As it happened, Cherry wanted to keep Cheevers in reserve for the Bruins' home game on Sunday night against Detroit, so Cheevers would dress as the backup for the Toronto game. It meant that goaltender Dave Reece was going to be in net, but I had no idea who he was until he showed up in the Boston goal for the opening faceoff.

Anyone who looks up Reece's record can see that he came into that game with a 7–4–2 won/lost mark with two shutouts and had been in goal when the Bruins beat Pittsburgh 5–1 in their game two nights earlier. The Penguins had a high-flying attack (second best in the NHL that season), so to hold them to one goal was a significant achievement for a 27-year-old rookie netminder. Boston's other goalie was Gilles Gilbert, but he was injured and unavailable. So was the great Bobby Orr, who made a difference in any game he ever played in; the superb defenceman was experiencing knee problems once again.

After leaving the Gardens following morning practice, I went about doing some errands. Traffic was bad around Toronto even back then, so it took me a lot longer than I wanted. Before going home, I picked up some chicken and fries on the spur of the moment. Believe it or not, I managed to eat the meal while still driving around! My wife, Wendy, wasn't home that day and I had to deal with my son, Ryan, who'd got himself dirty by falling in some mud. Despite my hectic day, I managed to get back to the Gardens in time for the game against the Bruins.

The first period ended with the Maple Leafs up 2–1 on goals by McDonald and Ian Turnbull. I assisted on both. Jean Ratelle got one back for Boston, but nothing unusual seemed at hand after one period. However, things started to happen early in the second period. Borje Salming led a rush into the Boston end and took a shot on net. I knocked the rebounding puck out of mid-air and past Reece for my first goal of the game. Then, off a draw in the Bruins' end, I got the puck back to Salming at the point. He drilled a shot past Reece to make it 4–1 on a power play. After Boston scored to close the gap, I came down the ice, just looking to get the puck in the Bruins' end on a line change. I put a slapshot on net and it knuckled past Reece for my fifth point of the night – and we hadn't even played half of the game yet!

"THOMPSON TO SITTLER, GOING RIGHT IN OVER THE LINE. SHOOTS . . . HE SCORES!"

Hockey Night in Canada's Bill Hewitt on Sittler's ninth point of the 10-point night

My second goal against the Bruins. ▶

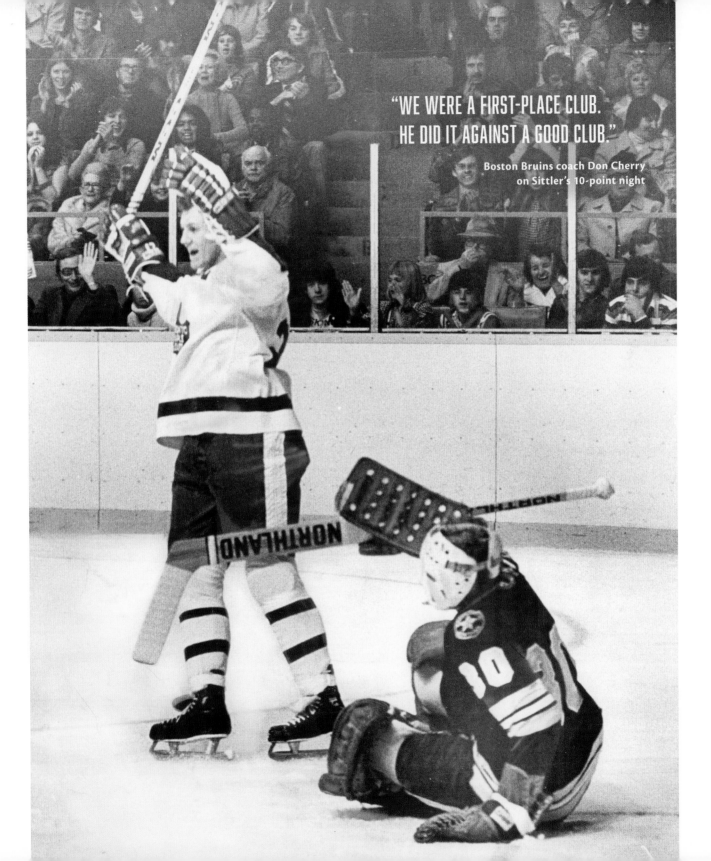

"WE WERE A FIRST-PLACE CLUB.
HE DID IT AGAINST A GOOD CLUB."

Boston Bruins coach Don Cherry
on Sittler's 10-point night

On another power-play chance, I took a nice pass from teammate Jack Valiquette right in the slot area and whipped it home for my third goal of the period. My second-period hat trick wasn't recognized with any tossed hats or caps, but I was sure having a good game. We were up 7–3 when Lanny and I helped set up Salming, who lunged for a loose puck and scored another goal that made it 8–3. Boston got one back to close the second period. It was 8–4 for the Maple Leafs, and I had seven points with a period still to play. At this point, I thought Cherry would signal for Cheevers to take over in net, but the Bruins goalie put a towel over his head and kept his head down. Goalies were not often pulled in this era, but I bet Reece was probably hoping for a little relief by the end of the second.

While we sat in the dressing room between periods, Toronto public relations director Stan Obodiac came in and said to me, "Darryl, I don't know if you are aware of this but you are one point away from the NHL record for most points in a game." Only two players, Maurice Richard (in 1944) and Bert Olmstead (in 1954), had eight-point games, while playing with the Montreal Canadiens. I was just one point shy of their mark. Now there was something to shoot for in the third period!

We started the final period on the power play, and Thompson and Salming made good passes to spring me loose down the wing. I went around Bruins defenceman Darryl Edestrand before cutting toward the net. I put a shot into the far corner just 44 seconds into the final frame to tie the NHL record. The Gardens crowd was going wild. One of those "charge" horns had been installed in the building, and it seemed to stir the fans to even greater heights. The flashing message boards at both ends of the arena – no replay screens in those days – kept the crowd informed of what was going on. I felt the energy.

Just before the middle of the period, I took a puck over the Boston blue line, but both Bruins defencemen (Dallas Smith and Gary Doak) backed away and left me an opening to split as Reece came out of his net. I let a shot go that caught the inside of the post, and it was in for a new NHL record: nine points in one game! The crowd was really loud now and loving every second of being a part of a historic night . . . and it wasn't over yet.

My last goal came from behind the Boston net when I was trying to hit Errol Thompson with a pass. The puck hit Brad Park of the Bruins in the skates and then deflected past Reece for the 10th point (and sixth goal, which came from 10 shots on net) of the evening. No player – not even the likes of Gordie Howe, Maurice Richard, Bobby Hull, Phil Esposito, or Guy Lafleur – had ever recorded 10 points in one game. In the 40 years that have passed since that night in 1976, greats such as Wayne Gretzky,

◀ The crowd at Maple Leaf Gardens responds to my great night.
I am at the end of the bench, next to Lanny.

Mario Lemieux, Alex Ovechkin, and Sidney Crosby have not been able to tie or break the mark. On 11 occasions since 1977, a player has recorded eight points in a game, but none has reached nine or 10. Maybe someone like Connor McDavid will do it one day, but it will be difficult – goal scoring is not as high today as it was in the 1970s and 1980s. (In 2014–15, no team scored 10 goals in a game – the closest was Nashville, with 9. As of January 1, 2016, no team has scored more than seven goals in one game during the 2015–16 campaign.) It is also interesting to note that it took 9,453 NHL games between the time the Rocket first recorded an eight-point game in 1944 to the time when I recorded 10 in 1976. Since that time over 39,000 NHL games (including games played in 2015–2016) have been played and nobody has tied or surpassed the mark.

"AS LONG AS HE LIVES, HE WILL REMEMBER THIS EVENING . . .
SO WILL ALL OF US DOING THIS GAME HERE AT MAPLE LEAF GARDENS."

Hockey Night in Canada's **Brian McFarlane after Sittler recorded his 10th point of the game**

As I look back at the 10-point night 40 years later, I realize I'm pretty lucky to have set that record and have it last all this time. These days, there probably would have been more fuss made about the game, but back then, there was no social media! Any fan who wants to see the highlights of that night needs to go on YouTube or track down a copy of a VHS tape made in 1989 by Molstar Productions entitled *Great Hockey Moments* (Volume 1). It shows each point while *HNIC* broadcaster Dick Irvin recounts the action. I have no way to account for what happened other than to say it was just a game where everything went my way, much as it did nearly three months later, when I scored five goals in one playoff game.

Sixth goal, 10th point. ▶

The 1976 playoffs had not gone very well for me heading into the sixth game of the Maple Leafs/Flyers series on April 22, 1976. We had eliminated the Pittsburgh Penguins 2–1 in the best-of-three opening round, but we were now down 3–2 to Philadelphia and I had only three assists to show for the first five contests. We needed to win this game at Maple Leaf Gardens or else it was time to go home again. The Flyers had wiped us out in four straight games in the 1975 post-season, but we were a much tougher team this time around.

"I WAS DOWN ON MYSELF BEFORE THE GAME. I WAS BOTHERED I WASN'T HELPING THE TEAM IN THE SCORING DEPARTMENT. BERNIE WAS STOPPING ME EARLIER IN THE SERIES AND HE IS STILL A GREAT GOALIE. HE JUST HAD A BAD NIGHT."

Darryl Sittler on his five-goal effort against Philadelphia

The series had been rough and controversial leading up to the sixth game of what was proving to be an extremely rugged matchup. In the third game of the series, the Flyers targeted our star defenceman Borje Salming and were able to isolate him during an all-out brawl. Borje took a severe beating from Mel Bridgman, one of the Flyers' many enforcers. There was no doubt Salming was being zeroed in on for special treatment, but Philadelphia realized the referees were not going to call everything (not in that era of hockey, which allowed for intimidation) and they took full advantage. Salming dusted himself off and scored a key goal in the next game to even the series at two games each. We lost the fifth game in Philadelphia by a 7–1 score but we were still confident we could send the series back to Philly for a deciding contest.

The Flyers scored first in game six, but I tied it when I batted in a loose puck. Then Thompson got one to give us a 2–1 lead after the first period. In the second I scored on a slapshot that went past Flyers goalie Bernie Parent just inside the post to give us a 3–1 lead. Then I rapped in a rebound of a Thompson

◀ **Celebrating my six goals.**

shot to make it 4–1 before Philadelphia got two back. However, before the second period was done, I took a long pass from defenceman Claire Alexander and broke in on Parent. I was tripped by defenceman Joe Watson, but as I was falling, I got a shot off that beat the Flyers' goalie. Parent had been a teammate on the Maple Leafs for a couple of seasons, though that provided no edge. I was shooting and the puck was going in the net. It was all done instinctively. We were now up 5–3.

In the third period I scored on a long shot that Parent misplayed. We were up 6–3 now and would go on to win 8–5. The five goals I scored tied an NHL playoff record for one game (which is shared with Newsy Lalonde, Maurice Richard, Reggie Leach, and Mario Lemieux), and an assist on a goal by Alexander gave me

"RED [KELLY] PUT A PYRAMID IN THE DRESSING ROOM YESTERDAY AFTERNOON. I PUT MY STICKS UNDERNEATH IT, HOPING IT MIGHT HELP. IT MIGHT HAVE HELPED AT THAT BUT I'M NOT A BELIEVER IN THE PYRAMID THEORY YET."

Darryl Sittler on Toronto coach Red Kelly's use of "pyramid power"

six points, equalling the NHL playoff mark held at the time by Dickie Moore and Phil Esposito (it has since been equalled and surpassed, with eight points now setting the new standard for a playoff game).

This was the same time that coach Red Kelly was fascinated with "pyramid power." I was always skeptical of that, but we did win the game, so who knows! Our fans were also very noticeable in this series. They let the Flyers know that their intimidating style of play was not liked in Toronto (or any other part of Canada, for that matter). The Maple Leafs were underdogs in this matchup and our fans knew it, so they were quite loud and boisterous. They gave the Flyers' bench a hard time – there was no glass between the fans and the team benches in 1976 – and kept it going when anyone was in the penalty box, which happened often over

We had many great battles with the Flyers in the mid-1970s. In action against Flyers' goalie ▶
Bernie Parent (top) and defenseman André "Moose" Dupont (bottom).

the course of the seven games (Philadelphia served 295 penalty minutes in this series; combined, the teams spent 525 minutes in the sin bin).

Flyers coach Fred Shero complained about the Toronto fans, as did a few of his players, but the very popular Maple Leafs had more than 16,000 fans on our side in every home game against Philadelphia. We didn't shrink away from the Flyers in this series like we had the year before. Guys such as Scott Garland, Kurt Walker, Tiger Williams, Dave Dunn, and Pat Boutette let the Flyers know this was going to be a tough battle. Our toughest players took on the fighting that had to be done, but I didn't have a single fight in the series. My role was to stay on the ice and create some offence, which we did quite well at the Gardens.

"I DON'T REALLY KNOW HOW TO DESCRIBE HOW I FEEL. I GUESS I FEEL LUCKY. I JUST DON'T KNOW WHY IT HAPPENED."

Darryl Sittler's post-game comments after his five goals in one playoff game versus the Flyers

---

Even though we were up 2–1 at the end of the first period in the seventh game, we ended up losing 7–3, which eliminated us from the playoffs. The Flyers were experienced and had won the Stanley Cup twice already. We were still young and not quite ready to take the defending champions out. We tried to use "pyramid power" for one more night by sitting under a large pyramid in our dressing room. It did not work out so well this time. It was a tough defeat for us to accept. I try to remember that even though Parent was not as sharp in the games played in Toronto, he was still one of the best goalies in hockey and almost unbeatable on home ice.

The summer of '76 was going to be a long one, since we were out before the month of May. Luckily, a new challenge came along – one that would make up for the loss to Philadelphia.

◀ **April 22: Celebrating my first goal.**

When the players were selected for the first Canada Cup tournament, to be played in September 1976, I was hoping to be one of those invited. My agent at the time was Alan Eagleson (who was also head of the NHLPA), and he was the main Canadian negotiator for this multi-nation tournament. He also had a voice in the selection of players. I think that helped to get me invited to training camp along with teammate Lanny McDonald, who was also an Eagleson client. It was made clear to us that even though 31 players had been chosen, there were going to be cuts before the start of the tournament.

I went to camp with the idea that I would do whatever was asked of me; if that meant playing out of position or accepting a different role, it was going to be fine by me. Lanny felt the same way. We were by no means sure we were going to make the final cut. Some other guys found it harder to accept roles that they were not used to and felt they should be treated like they were stars – which they obviously were on their respective NHL teams. Head coach Scotty Bowman was the man in charge, and all the players knew he was the one making the ultimate decisions. Lanny and I got slotted with Montreal's Bob Gainey, and we showed enough to make the team. This would be the first time I was going to represent my country as a hockey player, and it was a great thrill just to be named to the final roster. Six very good players were cut, and a few others did not play much, but we had a great team and were favoured to win it all – especially since most of the tournament would be played in Canada.

Our group was an interesting mix of young guys (Lanny, Marcel Dionne, Gilbert Perreault, Guy Lafleur, Denis Potvin, Larry Robinson, Bill Barber, Steve Shutt, and myself) and established veterans (Bobby Hull, Phil Esposito, Bobby Orr, Serge Savard, Guy Lapointe, and team captain Bobby Clarke). In total, 18 members of that team (including backup netminder Gerry Cheevers and coach Scotty Bowman) would be inducted into the Hockey Hall of Fame. Many players came from the Montreal Canadiens and the Philadelphia Flyers, which was understandable since they had met for the Stanley Cup in 1976, but the final group (featuring players from eight different teams plus Bobby Hull from the WHA's Winnipeg Jets) came together nicely, with all NHL team rivalries put aside for the good of the squad. We were going into this tournament very well prepared, unlike the 1972 Team Canada, which had had to learn and adjust on the fly.

The other five teams varied in strength, but the Soviets were ranked highly, with veterans from the '72 Summit Series on their roster, including Vladislav Tretiak in net and Alexander Maltsev at forward. The team from Czechoslovakia, led by Milan Novy, Ivan Hlinka, and two of the Stastny brothers –

Helping out Team Canada goalie Rogie Vachon at the Montreal Forum versus the Czech team (top); ▶
About to move in on Vladimír Dzurilla, the Czech netminder, to score my overtime winner (bottom).

27
1976 Canada Cup
Winning Goal
Sept 15/76

"THIS IS THE GREATEST
MOMENT OF MY LIFE.
NOT THE FACT THAT
I SCORED THE GOAL,
BUT THE FACT I WAS
ABLE TO PLAY."

**Darryl Sittler on being a member of
Team Canada in 1976, after scoring
the tournament-winning goal**

Marian and Peter – was also a strong entry. The team from Sweden would prove to be an entertaining and talented group, led by Borje Salming and Inge Hammarström from the Maple Leafs, along with others who played in North America, such as Thommie Bergman, Ulf Nilsson, Willy Lindström, and Anders Hedberg. Team USA was coached by Bob Pulford and Harry Neale and featured a lineup full of NHL players such as Mike Milbury, Lou Nanne, Craig Patrick, Robbie Ftorek, and Rick Chartraw. The team from Finland was less well known but had future NHL players such as Matti Hagman, Pekka Rautakallio, and goalie Markus Mattsson on the roster. Carl Brewer was one of the coaches for Finland.

Despite making the team, I wasn't sure I was going to be in the lineup every game. But Scotty Bowman liked the way I played and put me in for every game of the tournament, which I really appreciated. We lost only one game in the first round – a 1–0 thriller to the Czech team in Montreal – but won every other game we played to get to the final round, which would feature just two teams: Canada and Czechoslovakia (which at this point had not split into the Czech Republic and Slovakia). It was a best-of-three format for the final and we won the first game at Maple Leaf Gardens, 6–0. I scored the final goal of that game with just one second on the clock; it was my third of the tournament.

The second game was scheduled for September 15 at the Forum. The Czech squad was much better in this very well-played and exciting game. We were tied 4–4 at the end of regulation, which meant overtime under the tournament format. In the dressing room prior to the start of overtime, we talked about how Czech goalie Vladimír Dzurilla liked to come out of his net. The guys were saying that maybe if we held on to the puck for a second or two longer, we might be able to trap him in a bad spot. Assistant coach Don Cherry came into the room and told us he'd noticed the exact same thing, and that we might be able to go around the big goalie if we kept our heads up. You have to give Don credit for reminding us that this could be a way to score the winner.

We nearly scored on two occasions in the first 10-minute overtime session, but neither counted. As the second overtime began, I was out on a shift with Marcel Dionne and Lanny McDonald. Lanny got the puck to Marcel, who whipped a cross-ice pass over to me, and I went down the left wing. I managed to get past a Czech defenceman, which put me in alone. Dzurilla, who had played very well in this tournament, came out of his net, just as we had seen before. Instead of shooting, I held on to the puck while going wide. Dzurilla made a desperate lunge but it was too late – I was already past him. The net was wide open and I put it home to seal the first-ever Canada Cup tournament for Team Canada. The look on my face said it all, at least before I got mobbed by my teammates behind the net! I finished the tournament with four goals and two assists in seven games played and earned a spot on the tournament all-star team at forward.

Scoring the winning goal in the Canada Cup tournament capped off an incredible year; it's my favourite memory of 1976 because it came while playing for my country. Many people thank me for scoring that goal. Like Paul Henderson's famous goal versus the Soviets, or Sidney Crosby's golden goal at the Winter Olympic Games, it secured a victory for Canada. Playing in the 1976 Canada Cup was the highlight of my career. Being a Stanley Cup winner is the only thing that might have come close.

METRO WEATHER
intermittent rain tomorrow, high 18 Celsius. Low tonight 15C. Details page A2.

ESTABLISHED 1892

August paid circulation Mon.-Fri. 474,913; Sat. 740,527

The Toronto Star

four star
★★★★
edition

Thursday, September 16, 1976—90 pages

Monday-Friday 15c; Saturday 35c; Home delivery $1

Champagne-soaked Darryl Sittler: 'What a year!'

By FRANK ORR
Star staff writer

MONTREAL — There simply can't be many big nights left for Darryl Sittler in 1976. The way the Maple Leaf centre views it, he's just about used up his quota for this year and even a few years in the future.

Sittler's latest extravaganza came at 11.33 of overtime at the Forum here last night when he scored the winning goal for Team Canada in a 5-4 victory over the Czechoslovakian national team. That gave the Canadians the best-of-three final in the six-nation tournament in two straight games.

The goal, which ended a wild, frantic ultra-exciting hockey match, is added to Sittler's other two "big evenings" this year — his 10-point effort against Boston Bruins in February and his April special, a five-goal playoff game against Philadelphia Flyers.

"What a year," Sittler said, clutching a bottle of champagne in the uproarious Team Canada dressing room.

"How do you explain one guy having a year like I've had? The big nights just came my way for some reason which I'll never be able to explain. They've all been incredible, all big thrills, but there was something pretty special about this one, scoring a goal that won a world championship for a team representing your country. Not much could top that, could it?"

Sittler could explain the reasons for his score. A tip from Team Canada coach Don Cherry, one of the four-man staff, was behind it.

"Don Cherry had noticed that Vladimir Dzurilla, the Czech goalie who was giving us trouble, was moving out, way out, of the net and we were helping him by shooting too quickly," Sittler said.

"As a result, many of our shots, especially s o m e good chances by Bobby Hull and Steve Shutt, were just bouncing off him as he cut down the angle. Cherry suggested that we hold on to the puck a little longer until he did move out and we'd have some daylight to shoot at. That's what I did. I held it until I was in pretty deep, he came out and there was a hole on the far side.

"I shot for it and in it went. I don't remember too much of what happened in the next few minutes because everything went a little crazy. I guess I knew things were over when I saw Alan Eagleson (the tournament chairman) running towards me down the ice."

● The party's over for Team Canada's players—but they all agree it was great — while it lasted. Full coverage of last night's game, pages C1, C2 and C3.

18

"HOW DO YOU EXPLAIN ONE GUY HAVING A YEAR LIKE I'VE HAD? THE BIG NIGHTS JUST CAME MY WAY FOR SOME REASON WHICH I'LL NEVER BE ABLE TO EXPLAIN. THEY'VE ALL BEEN INCREDIBLE, ALL BIG THRILLS, BUT THERE WAS SOMETHING PRETTY SPECIAL ABOUT THIS ONE, SCORING A GOAL THAT WON A WORLD CHAMPIONSHIP FOR A TEAM REPRESENTING YOUR COUNTRY. NOT MUCH COULD TOP THAT, COULD IT?"

Darryl Sittler, September 15, 1976

When hockey fans talk about the three big moments I had in 1976, they tend to talk more about the 10-point night against Boston. Maybe that's because the game versus the Bruins was on national television, and the record has not been tied or surpassed. Also, tournaments like the Canada Cup or the Olympic Games are events that happen every four years, and then those memories get put away until the next time, although one estimate of the television audience for the last game of the Canada Cup in 1976 was 10.7 million. Whatever the reason, the 10-point night still resonates with hockey fans more than any other moment.

The year 2016 marked the 40th anniversary of that magical 1976. Even though that seems like a long time ago, it sometimes feels to me almost as if time has stood still – even when I talk to people who weren't around in '76. One of the main reasons I decided to put this book together was to commemorate those three special moments in my hockey career. I hope you will enjoy reading it as much as I've enjoyed reliving all these wonderful memories.

TWO

FROM ST. JACOBS TO LONDON

FAMILY LIFE

My grandfather Jacob Sittler had 12 children, so there was always lots of family around while I was growing up. Jacob, who was born in 1900, was my minor hockey coach in pee wee and bantam. He was also a milkman. I recall going on his route with him on many occasions. He was a strong man who outlived seven of his children, including my dad. My family bought Jacob's house when all the other kids had gone.

My mom and dad were hard-working people who did the best they could while raising a large family. They both thought it was important to go to church and be in the choir, so that's what we did. My mom, Doris, had three kids by the time she was just 20 years old (and eight in total), which kept her quite busy. My dad, Ken, had a good job working as a crane operator and volunteered to help out with hockey wherever he could. I quickly learned that the best way to get something was to work for it, so I would take any job available: delivering newspapers, cutting grass, shovelling snow, helping out on farms, sweeping the main street in St. Jacobs – whatever it took to earn money.

St. Jacobs was a Mennonite town and many people in the community used a horse and buggy to get around, which meant that the streets were filled with manure. My brother Ken and I had steady work (at 75 cents an hour) shovelling the main street on a Saturday morning! On occasion we were able to use the money we earned to buy hockey equipment. Whatever we chose was always treasured since such items were not easy to get for us – especially anything brand new.

Both of my parents were very supportive and drove us everywhere to play hockey or softball. Sports were a big part of life in St. Jacobs. If we won a championship, we got to ride in the volunteer fire truck down the main street, from one end of town to the other. We were thrilled to do it. It was all part of a very happy childhood that included watching *Hockey Night in Canada* (we had a TV with a bunny-ear antenna!). We would get ready to watch our favourite show every Saturday night by taking a bath and then enjoying a treat like chips or popcorn or some pop. The whole family would gather around and I remember it as a good time. There were also a lot of family outings that involved fishing and camping since my father was an avid fisherman. I came to love fishing as well, and landing a big one was always

◀ **Left to right, back row: my brothers Gary and Ken; my mother and father, Doris and Ken; me; my grandparents, Frances and Jacob; left to right, front row: my brothers Jeff and Rod, my sisters, Debbie and Linda; my brother Tim; and Claude, in about 1970!**

very exciting. Many of our family vacations were based on getting the car to a good spot and then enjoying the hunting, fishing, and camping.

One of the biggest influences in my early years was my Uncle Tom, my father's youngest brother. He was about seven years older than I was, and always seemed more like an older brother than an uncle. We both liked the same things – fishing, hockey, and playing catch – and he would take me places. He had more free time and was more available to me than my dad, who had to work, so we became very close. Uncle Tom had a warm personality and I enjoyed his company very much. It didn't hurt that he was a very good local hockey player. He took great interest in the sport, like I did, and I think he might have been good enough to become a professional player. He worked hard to stay in shape by running. I always looked up to him.

When Uncle Tom was 21 he was killed in a car accident – the first traumatic event in my life. I was 13 or 14 at the time and I cried many tears. I vowed that I would dedicate myself to his memory in everything I did. I would never quit anything because it would let my Uncle Tom down. I would persevere and be persistent to honour him. It was a source of motivation that I kept between myself and Uncle Tom.

As far as hockey was concerned, I was able to play in one of the many outdoor rinks we had near home. There were always lots of kids around, and after school it was time to drop the books, get out on the ice, and just play. Sometimes we had to shovel snow to get some clean ice – not that we minded. If we played late into the night we would turn on the floodlights. It was on these outdoor rinks that I worked on my skating and learned to turn in both directions. I also worked on my game by playing ball hockey. My brother Gary and I pushed each other to compete as hard as possible.

I played organized hockey in nearby Elmira, Ontario. I was able to play house league and with a travelling team. You were allowed to play up a level, too, which meant that in one year I could play on as many as four different teams, with the games scheduled one right after the other. Playing on so many teams is no longer allowed, but it was great for my development back then. I was on teams that did well at the annual pee wee tournament in Goderich, Ontario, and at the tournament held during the Elmira Maple Syrup Festival. We wore yellow hockey jackets and then added cheap purple fedoras to make us really stand out! We thought it was a cool thing to do. I also remember a trip we took to Washington, DC, to play teams there. We got to see the White House. These were great experiences for a youngster.

(Clockwise) My siblings. Back row: me, Linda, and Ken, and ▶ front row: Debbie and Gary; Me, age two, with my dad; My grandfather Jacob was a milkman in St. Jacobs, Ontario.

But there was also some disappointment. When I was 15 and playing midget hockey, a spot opened up on the Junior C team in Elmira. It was between me and another boy. We were pretty evenly matched in terms of skill and talent, but they chose him. I was heartbroken, to say the least, but I went back to midget and captained a team that went deep into the playoffs. I recall scoring a bunch of goals in the Ontario midget finals, although I think we lost the last game. Meanwhile, the Elmira Junior C team was out of the playoffs, so it turned out pretty well for me.

The next year, when I was 16, I went to play for the Elmira juniors, which put me up against some 19-year-olds. It was hard but I did pretty well and was a league leader in scoring. The London Junior A team was scouting me at the time but I was hoping the Kitchener Rangers of the Ontario Hockey League (OHL) would have interest as well. St. Jacobs is much closer to Kitchener, and that would have made things easier for my family. The Rangers had a better team, though, so I knew it would be difficult to crack that lineup, which featured guys like future NHL star Walter Tkaczuk.

Even though Kitchener was just down the road from my house, it was better for my development to play in London. Mom and Dad would make the hour-and-fifteen-minute trek to London even during the week, when work might not end until five o'clock. They were proud of me and I appreciated their efforts to come watch me play. I was one of the very few guys (Rod Seiling, who was from Elmira, was another player who also made it to the NHL) from the area who was playing Junior A hockey, so it was something special. My brothers and sisters would also get dragged along from time to time, but that was part of being a family.

As for other sports, I was a good softball pitcher and I would practise a lot, just like I did with hockey. With so many brothers around there was always someone to play with and practise developing skills. If I had to do something alone I did not mind that either because I knew it was going to help me to get better. I ran track and field and did cross-country at school, but for me that was all about preparing for hockey. I also knew I had to "get by" academically, and that's how I approached schoolwork, which is why I had marks in the 60 to 65 range. I know I would have been a better student if I'd put in more effort but my focus was on hockey. As I kept moving up, I could see that I was competitive and able to keep up at every stage. I was an all-star selection at various levels, which helped me to see that a career in hockey might be possible. In fact, I was sure of it!

The London team drafted me third overall in 1967, and in June of that year, coach Turk Broda came to our house. I remember he drove up in his big Cadillac. My dad was all excited – Turk had been

My Uncle Tom. ▶

a legendary goalie for the Maple Leafs, and it was a big thing that he was coming over to see our family. Turk took us out for a pigtails-and-sauerkraut dinner at the Breslau Hotel. When we got home he said to my parents – pointing his finger for emphasis – "I will make your son a hockey player." Turk was replaced after my first season in London but he certainly got me off in the right direction for the first season. In 2016, Turk was named to Maple Leafs Legends Row, so it will be nice to have his statue close to mine.

My parents, who had never pushed me to pursue hockey, knew it would be hard for me to leave home, but they did not discourage me in any way. I knew the OHL was my best chance for making it to the NHL. Ohio's Bowling Green University was offering me a hockey scholarship, but watching OHL teams like the Kitchener Rangers, Toronto Marlies, and Hamilton Red Wings convinced me this was the way to go. On Labour Day weekend of 1967, with my dad working, my mom drove me to London Gardens with my suitcase packed. We met the London Nationals general manager and then it was off to my billet. My mother said goodbye and drove home on what was a beautiful late summer day. A couple of days later it was off to my new high school, H.B. Beal Secondary, and then to hockey practice the next day. That month, I turned 17.

Ball hockey with my brothers – Tim, in goal, Rod, and Jeff (top); ▶
With Turk Broda, and Don Culbert, Rick Falk, and Don Carter,
at my first practice with the London Nationals (bottom).

FIRST IMPRESSIONS

Growing up in a small Mennonite town like St. Jacobs, Ontario, was tough on a hockey fan. My parents could never get tickets to a Maple Leafs game in Toronto. One year, though, my dad did manage to get tickets for a pre-season NHL game in nearby Kitchener, between the New York Rangers and the Chicago Black Hawks.

   I was about 10 years old at the time. On a cold September night, I waited outside the arena after the game hoping to catch a glimpse of an NHL star, and maybe score an autograph. Chicago's Bobby Hull and New York's Andy Bathgate both signed my piece of paper. I brought my autographs to school, and by using some tracing paper, I was able to copy the signatures and give them to my friends.

"HE SIGNED IT AND RUFFLED MY HAIR. ALL THE WAY HOME I KEPT LOOKING AT BOBBY HULL'S AUTOGRAPH. IT WAS ONE OF THE HAPPIEST DAYS OF MY LIFE."

Darryl Sittler, *Maple Leaf Magazine*, October 14, 1978

   I have retold this story at many events, and one time, in British Columbia, Bobby Hull was with me. After telling the audience how I secured Hull's signature, Bobby gave me an approving tap and a smile. I have never forgotten getting those autographs, and I always do my best to sign whenever I am asked. You only get one chance to make a first impression, and everyone can decide if it is going to be good, bad, or indifferent.

◀ Darryl and Bobby Hull at Team Canada training camp in September 1976 (left).
Andy Bathgate, who died in 2016, was the Rangers' best player and became team captain (right).

JEAN BÉLIVEAU

Most kids have a favourite player growing up. My hockey hero was Jean Béliveau of the Montreal Canadiens. My dad and my brothers were Maple Leafs fans, but I liked the way the Canadiens played the game, and Béliveau was a talented centre who could score goals. I also played centre and loved to score, so it seemed natural for me to like a player such as Béliveau. I also liked listening to Danny Gallivan doing the play-by-play of the Montreal games on *Hockey Night in Canada*. The Habs were a very successful team at that time and it seemed like they won the Stanley Cup every year.

One Christmas I got a Montreal Canadiens sweater with number 4 on the back, just like Béliveau had on his jersey. I wore it everywhere. Years later, as a rookie with the Maple Leafs in 1970–71, I faced-off against him during games at Maple Leaf Gardens and the Montreal Forum. That season was Béliveau's last in the NHL, and it was a surreal experience for me to play against him. I was in awe.

As the years went by I got to know and talk to Jean Béliveau at various NHL and Hockey Hall of Fame events. In May 2008, Béliveau was inducted into the YM-YWHA Alex Dworkin Montreal Jewish Sports Hall of Fame. He was the first non-Jewish athlete to be inducted. Former NHL players were invited, and Johnny Bower and I went as representatives of the Toronto Maple Leafs.

When my wife, Wendy, died, Béliveau called me on the morning of her funeral. He reached me at my home in East Amherst, New York, to say he was thinking of me on a very difficult day. I'm not even certain how he got my number. I attended his funeral in Montreal when he died in 2014.

My favourite Maple Leafs as a kid were goalie Johnny Bower and defenceman Tim Horton. During the '71 playoffs we had a couple of big brawls in one game in New York against the Rangers. At one point I wanted to go over and help out a teammate who was having some trouble, but Horton, who was a Ranger by this time, just grabbed my arms and said, "You're not going anywhere." I think I said, "Yes, sir." He was 41 years old at the time and I was a big, strong kid of 21, but I tell you I did not move! Stories of Horton's legendary strength were absolutely true.

◀ Jean Béliveau had a very classy and regal style about him. Here, the legendary
Hall of Fame member waves to the crowd while Johnny Bower and I applaud.

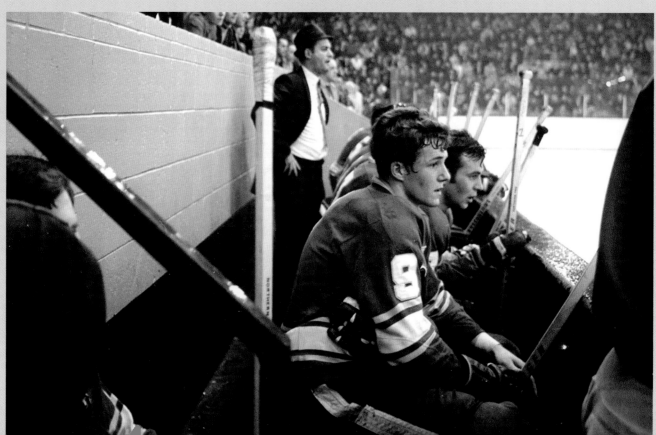

JUNIOR HOCKEY

The OHL did a great job developing players for the NHL, and my experience was no exception. Going up against players like Phil Roberto, Don Lever, Rick MacLeish, Marcel Dionne, Dale Tallon, Gilbert Perreault, Rick Martin, Denis Potvin, and Terry O'Reilly (all of whom made it to the big leagues), among many others, helped prepare me for the next step, which came when I graduated high school after three years in London.

Back then, the coaches didn't emphasize systems. We just played the games, and practice consisted of scrimmages plus shooting and skating drills. In addition to Turk Broda, my other coaches in London were Gene Taylor and Armand "Bep" Guidolin. Joining the London team in 1967–68 worked out well for me, since a few of their better players – such as Garry Unger and Walt McKechnie – were centres who had graduated. Their departure left a void for me to fill, and I recorded 63 points (22 came on goals) in 54 games played as a rookie for the London Nationals.

During my first summer in London, I was asked to be an instructor at the summer hockey school run by the team, which was now known as the London Knights. Some NHL players (such as Dean Prentice and Darryl Edestrand) were also instructors, and when we got the ice to ourselves in the evening, I realized I could keep up with these guys. I started working at developing my body by lifting weights and by taking a job where I had to mix cement and sand for the construction of swimming pools. I also joined a rowing club, knowing that such exercise allows you to develop everything you need to be physically fit and build endurance. During my time in junior, I went from 165 to 195 pounds. I was more ready than I'd ever been for the rigours of the NHL.

I was named team captain for the start of my second season in London, which was an honour. It was also good experience, as I learned "on the job" how to keep a team together through a number of changes. It was good preparation for what I would deal with years later as captain of the Maple Leafs! I also put up my best junior numbers that season, with 34 goals and 99 points in 53 games. I had a five-goal game against Niagara Falls, and a local jeweller commemorated the occasion with a ring featuring the Knights logo and five diamonds.

◀ **In action for the London Knights (top); On the London Knights bench (bottom).**

It wasn't all good news, though. I injured my knee that season, and worried that the damage might hurt my career. Thankfully, we had a really good hospital in London, with some terrific doctors like Dr. Jack Kennedy and Dr. Peter Fowler – two of the top orthopaedic surgeons in Canada and pioneers in the field of sports medicine. Even so, I had to wear a custom-designed knee brace (made famous by NFL quarterback Joe Namath and designed by the Lenox Hill Brace Shop in New York) for the rest of my career, and I put in plenty of time rehabbing the injury.

Back in that era, good players were always targeted. I remember one game when Tony Featherstone of the Peterborough Petes jumped me when he came out of the penalty box and we went at it. Steve Durbano of the Toronto Marlies was a very wild guy. He locked horns with almost everybody (including me), as his 371 penalty minutes in 1969–70 indicate! The best players had to defend themselves; if you could show you could handle the tough going, the opposition might think twice about coming after you. I had 126 penalty minutes my third year in London but still managed to score 42 times.

After Grade 12, I went to Fanshawe College and eventually settled on a construction technology program. I liked working with my hands and had plenty of experience in this area since my dad had always been one to fix and repair things. I was good enough to get passing grades and tried to be responsible about school, but as always, my focus was on hockey.

Even though I didn't put a lot of effort into being a top student, I believe I would have found a way to be successful no matter what I tried. I had discipline and worked hard, and was highly motivated to do well regardless of the path I chose. I have said many times that I most likely would have been a crane operator like my father. However, my passion was to be a hockey player, and as I grew I was always among the best players. I knew that you have to work for everything and that nobody was going to hand me anything, but I believed I was ready for the challenge of playing in the National Hockey League.

It seems I was ready for other challenges too. Before I got to London, I'd had a casual girlfriend, but nothing serious. A friend of mine named Barry Boughner who was also at H.B. Beal Secondary introduced me to a very beautiful blonde named Wendy Bibbings. Wendy's family lived in London and came to many of our games. We got engaged in 1970 and married on June 5, 1971, following my rookie year in the NHL.

Our wedding day – June 5, 1971 (top); ▶
With my grandfather Jacob and my father, Ken (bottom).

THREE

THE ROOKIE

FIRST CONTRACT

This photo with Maple Leafs general manager Jim Gregory was taken in September of 1970, just before my first NHL training camp. In those days juniors were not drafted until they turned 20. There was no combine to assess skill and athletic ability and there were no interviews with NHL teams. I had no idea the Leafs were especially interested in me but Jimmy Tye, a local scout for the team, knew me from my minor hockey days. Tye knew my family and stayed in touch with my mom. Mom told me about him but I didn't pay much attention to it. Gilbert Perreault and Dale Tallon were going to be drafted by the expansion teams in Buffalo and Vancouver; after that nothing was assured.

On the day of the draft – June 11, 1970 – I was working at my summer job (installing swimming pools). Later on, while driving in the truck with the radio breaking up, came the news that I'd been selected by the Maple Leafs eighth overall. Boston took Reggie Leach and Rick MacLeish. Montreal drafted goalie Ray Martyniuk and forward Chuck Lefley. Pittsburgh picked Greg Polis from Estevan, Saskatchewan, and then the Leafs took me.

There was no big press conference and no sweater and ball cap waiting for me. At some point, though, my agent was called and the Leafs signed me for two years at $15,000 per season ($9,000 and then $10,000 if I played in the minors) plus a $10,000 signing bonus to be paid over two instalments ($7,500 in year one and $2,500 in year two).

The 1970 Amateur Draft saw 115 players selected (109 Canadians and six Americans). Only two made it to the Hockey Hall of Fame – Gilbert Perreault and me.

"I WAS AMAZED AND DELIGHTED THAT HE WAS STILL FREE WHEN WE GOT OUR FIRST PICK AFTER SEVEN OTHERS HAD BEEN CHOSEN. I THOUGHT HE'D GO IN THE FIRST FIVE OR SIX. HE'S A GOOD CENTRE, BIG, MEAN, CAN MAKE PLAYS AND SCORE GOALS."

Maple Leafs general manager Jim Gregory on selecting Darryl Sittler in 1970

◄ With Jim Gregory.

NUMBER 27

The very first time I walked into the Leafs dressing room at Maple Leaf Gardens, I was escorted by general manager Jim Gregory. It was September 1970, and as we made our way through the big wooden door into the room, Gregory told me where I would be sitting. I looked over at the stall and saw sweater number 27. It's something I will always remember. I knew the history of the Leafs, and that Frank Mahovlich had worn that number during the glory days of the 1960s. It made me realize quite quickly that they expected big things from me. I hadn't asked for any particular number, so it was an honour to be given this one.

Since that time, number 27 has been a part of so many important events in my life. My grandson Sawyer was born on February 27, and the date of my 10-point night in 1976 was February 7 – month two, day seven. My Hockey Hall of Fame induction year, 1989, adds up to 27, as does my birthday (September 18).

Frank Mahovlich wore number 27 for the Maple Leafs, and helped lead Toronto to four ▶
Stanley Cups (left). The first Leafs sweater I put on was just like the ones the team had worn
during its 1967 Stanley Cup victory. I wore it for just one game in my rookie year of
1970–71 – the season opener in Vancouver – before we switched to new uniforms (right).

ROOKIE YEAR

In this photo I am with Brian Marchinko, on the left, and Bob Liddington, on the right, with me in the middle. Marchinko and Liddington were both signed as free agents in 1969 after junior careers in Western Canada. Marchinko was a teammate of mine with the London Nationals in 1967–68.

The three of us were all rookies at the Leafs training camp in September 1970. Liddington was a nice kid from Alberta; the six-foot-tall left-winger made the team to start the season. I will always remember when we were out in New Brunswick to play our first pre-season game. Liddington and I were approached by a young fan at the airport who asked for our autographs. A group of young kids had played hooky from school to greet the Maple Leafs and they were getting autographs from Dave Keon, Norm Ullman, Ron Ellis, and other well-known guys. When Bob and I signed for this kid, he read the signatures and said, "Ah, they're nobodies." I can still see him tearing up the paper! Sometimes I wonder if he wishes he'd kept those autographs.

Liddington played 11 career games for the Leafs, all in 1970–71, and recorded one assist. Marchinko, a six-foot-tall centre/right-winger from Saskatchewan, played in two games in that first season and then another three for Toronto in 1971–72. Liddington moved to the World Hockey Association (WHA) while Marchinko played 42 career games for the New York Islanders.

Brian Marchinko, me, and Bob Liddington. ▶

41

FIRST GOAL

On the night of Saturday, November 28, 1970, the Detroit Red Wings were in town. It was our 21st game of the season and I had not yet scored a goal. I was on for a five-on-three power play in the first period, but still no goal, although we were up 3–0 at the end of the frame. During the intermission I was the guest of Ward Cornell – my first interview on *Hockey Night in Canada* – and I knew my family back home would be watching. I was very nervous, but Cornell was a nice man who put me at ease.

"SITTLER FIRED A TREMENDOUS SHOT." **TV analyst Bob Goldham on Sittler's goal**

We covered a number of items during the few minutes we spoke, including my education, switching from centre to left wing, preparing myself for the NHL, and how some of my veteran teammates were helping me out. When Cornell asked about my NHL ambition, I quickly said I wanted to score my first goal. He replied that a player's first appearance on *HNIC* usually led to a goal. "Good luck to you, Darryl," he said, closing the interview.

Nothing happened in the second period, but with the Leafs leading 6–1, Detroit made a change for the start of the third, removing goalie Roy Edwards for Don "Smokey" McLeod, who was playing in his first NHL game. At the 1:41 mark of the final period, defenceman Jim McKenny sent a long pass to Mike Walton, who slid a backhand over to me. I let a shot go from about 40 feet out, right along the ice, and beat McLeod through the pads. Usually a teammate will retrieve the puck for you after a special goal, but I was right there all alone and so excited that I picked it up myself. I was so happy to get that first one! I added an assist on a goal by Ron Ellis to cap off a 9–4 win and a great day for me.

My *HNIC* interview with Ward Cornell (top); ▶
Celebrating my first goal, which was also the first allowed by Don McLeod in the NHL (bottom).

"HE GOT THE WORD FROM WARD." **TV broadcaster Bill Hewitt after Sittler's first goal**

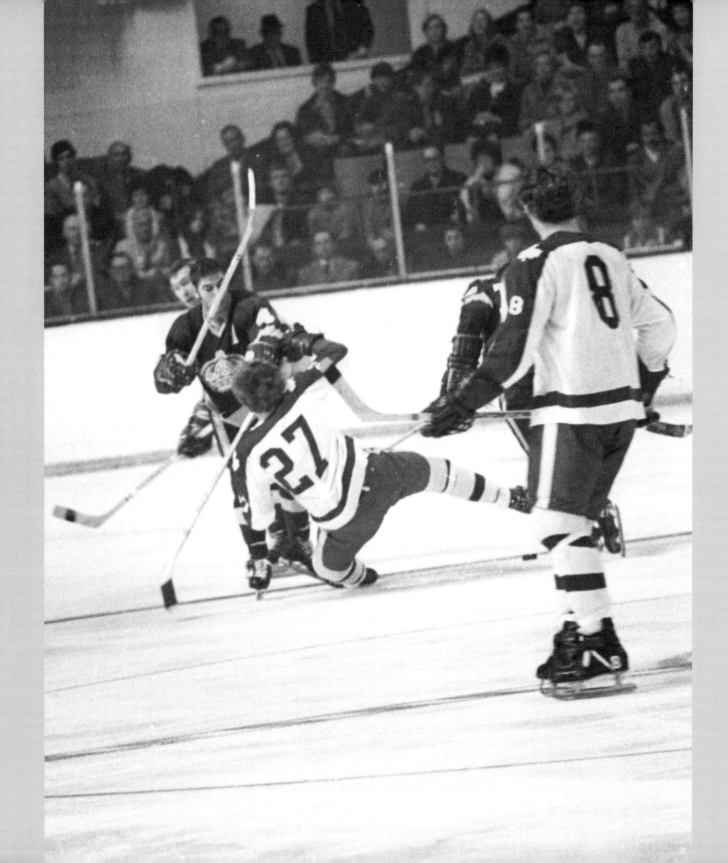

THE BROKEN WRIST

During my rookie season, the Los Angeles Kings were in town for a game on January 16, 1971. Toronto won easily by a score of 8–1, but in the third period I was taking the puck through the centre-ice area when I ran into a cement block named Gilles Marotte. Solid at five foot nine and 205 pounds, Marotte could catch forwards with their heads down and do some damage. It was best to stay away from the man known as "Captain Crunch," but I had a lapse in memory and it cost me. The Los Angeles defenceman caught me with a body check. I tried to get my arms up to protect myself, but something went wrong. My left arm did not go back properly, and my hand had moved over into a crooked position.

I was taken to the hospital where it was discovered that I had about 14 small bone fractures in my wrist. The doctor managed to put everything back in place, and avoid surgery, but I needed to wear a cast for more than two months. I was out until late March, and once I returned I had to wear a brace for the next two years. I spent time rebuilding the strength in my wrist through rehabilitation and exercises, but it took about two seasons to get my shot back to where it had been. Luckily, the injury didn't require screws or a hinge, and even today I have no arthritis pain in the joint, although the flexibility there is not the same as in my other arm. My rookie season was reduced to 49 games, but all things considered I was pretty lucky. In January 2016, my 11-year-old grandson, Luke, broke his wrist when he fell off his skateboard. I told Luke his wrist will heal, and he will get better just like I did.

◀ The Gilles Marotte hit that led to a wrist injury in my rookie year.

BOBBY BAUN AND JIM HARRISON

Defenceman Bobby Baun returned to the Maple Leafs early in the 1970–71 season and the veteran (who had won four Stanley Cups with Toronto in the 1960s) stabilized our blue line, which was very young at the time with the likes of Mike Pelyk, Jim Dorey, Rick Ley, Brad Selwood, Jim McKenny, and Brian Glennie. On the ice Baun showed me how forwards like me are eliminated by big, tough defencemen.

Off the ice I quickly learned that Baun had a strong appreciation for the finer things in life such as high-end cars and smoking quality cigars. On a trip out to Vancouver when he was my roommate, Baun went out one afternoon and bought a whalebone Inuit carving for $5,000. That amount represented a full third of my salary as a rookie! I was a young kid from a small town so that was a real eye opener for me but I've always liked hanging out with "Boomer."

Another player I hung out with in my rookie year was centre Jim Harrison. I was a bachelor in my first NHL season and he was one of the guys who made me most welcome. He and his wife sort of looked after me, and Jim was the first player to ask me to come along for a beer with the other guys on the team. We both loved fishing and hunting, so that gave us something in common. We were also roommates on the road for a while. On the ice we often played on the same line for the first two years but I actually got a break when Harrison jumped to the World Hockey Association in 1972 because that opened up a spot at centre for me. It was at that point that I became a productive player for the Maple Leafs. Harrison played in the WHA with the Alberta Oilers and is the only other professional hockey player to record a 10-point night – he scored three goals and added seven assists on January 30, 1973, in a game against the New York Raiders.

"WE WERE REALLY CLOSE. I USED TO LOOK AFTER HIM WHEN HE BROKE IN WITH THE LEAFS." **Jim Harrison on Darryl Sittler**

**Bobby Baun versus Bobby Clarke (top); Jim Harrison and I attack the ▶
New York Rangers' net in the 1971 playoffs (bottom).**

"I LIKED TO GIVE SITTLER A ROUGH TIME IN PRACTICE. I'D PUT MY STICK BETWEEN HIS LEGS TO PULL HIM DOWN AND THAT WOULD ANNOY HIM TO NO END. HE'D GET HIS REVENGE WHEN HE GOT BACK TO HIS FEET BY RUBBING MY BALD HEAD. THAT WAS JUST AS HARD FOR ME TO BEAR." **Bobby Baun**

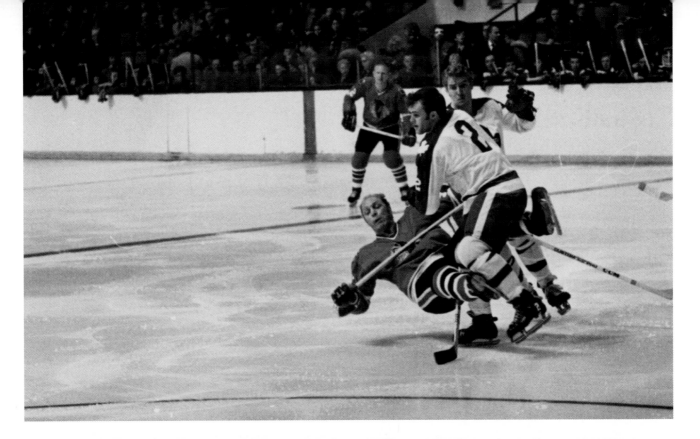

BRIAN SPENCER

It is amazing to think that Brian Spencer made it all the way from the very remote British Columbia town of Fort St. James to the NHL. Spencer was drafted by the Maple Leafs in 1969 and played in nine games for Toronto in 1969–70. Since we both had big curly hair, we were often mistaken for each other – I can recall owner Harold Ballard calling me "Spinner" (Brian's nickname) on more than one occasion. Spencer was sent back to Tulsa at the start of my rookie year. Brian was a very hungry player and he got called back early in the year, recording 24 points in 50 games. He was a very likeable guy but he also had a very short fuse that could go off at any time.

In December 1970, Brian's father was killed by the RCMP when he refused to put a weapon down and opened fire. Roy Spencer was trying to get a CBC affiliate station in British Columbia to change their broadcast to the Leafs game on a Saturday night. Brian was interviewed by Ward Cornell that night during our game against Chicago. Amazingly, Brian played the next night in Buffalo and I can still recall Jim Gregory telling a group of us what had transpired as we joined the team bus in Mississauga. I also remember that Brian was on the bus.

Many years later I saw Brian in a Florida prison, where he was awaiting trial on a murder charge. I drove across Florida to see him, but because he had only half an hour of visitation time, he had to see me, his mother, and his twin brother, Byron, all once. Brian was eventually found not guilty, and I tried to help him get back to Canada when he expressed an interest in coming back here at a lunch meeting in Toronto. I urged him not to go back to Florida, where he lived in a trailer, but he did return to his previous life. He was shot and killed in Florida in June 1988 – dead at the age of 38. It was a sad ending for a guy who had come so far to play in the NHL.

◀ Brian Spencer looks on as Bobby Hull is knocked down by Rick Ley. (top)

◀ The Maple Leafs team photo for the 1971–72 season, which was used on the Maple Leaf Gardens Christmas card. Jacques Plante, Ron Ellis, Norm Ullman, Dave Keon, Paul Henderson, and Bernie Parent are all in this photo, from my first year in the league. I am in the last row, third from the right, and Brian Spencer is next to me, second in and standing next to Jim Harrison. As you can see, Brian and I did look quite a bit alike. Spencer had 223 points in 553 career games – pretty good for a player who was known more for his toughness than anything else (bottom).

AN ENDORSEMENT DEAL TO REMEMBER

Very early in my career, my agent, Alan Eagleson, made me a part of a group of players who were endorsing hockey equipment and products made by CCM. As part of the deal each player had to agree to do signings. One day, I was sent to the Eaton's store on College Street in Toronto. I was just getting started in my career, and hardly anyone turned out to get my autograph, but I still sat there for the full two hours as I was obligated to do. While I was there, I struck up a conversation with a young guy wearing a navy-blue sports jacket. He was working at the store, stocking shelves. This young man turned out to be John Candy, who became very famous as a comedic actor on television and in movies.

Years later, while Candy was working at *SCTV*, he mimicked a young version of me when the comedy troupe did a takeoff of the Canadian hockey movie *Face-Off*, a film starring Art Hindle and Trudy Young. I appeared in the movie, as did many other Maple Leafs who were on the 1971 team. In the spoof, which they called "Power Play," Candy got my hair and look just right, and he captured my mannerisms as well. Later on I got to meet many of the other *SCTV* actors, including Eugene Levy, Andrea Martin, and Martin Short. I was "interviewed" at Casino Rama by Short, who was acting as Jiminy Glick, one of the characters he created. I thought it was very funny.

One of the first endorsement deals I received when I came to the NHL was from CCM. Here, I'm using one of their sticks; John Candy (above) in the blue and white sweater of the "Bay Leaves." His character in the SCTV "Movie of the Week" was known as "Billy Stemhovlichski," but he was really playing me (in fact, the credits list Darryl Sittler as Billy). On the left is Rick Moranis, who plays a George Armstrong–type character as captain of the team.

NORM ULLMAN

Along with Dave Keon, Jim Harrison, and Mike Walton, Norm Ullman was one of the Maple Leafs' veteran centres when I joined the club. He was a very intense and consistent player, and a very humble person. Most of his time as a Leaf was spent centring one of the best lines in the NHL, with Ron Ellis and Paul Henderson. Having so many quality centres meant I had to play on left wing for a couple of seasons, but it was great having guys like Ullman around to show me the ropes.

"I NEVER SAW A ROOKIE WORK THIS HARD." **Norm Ullman on Darryl Sittler**

One of my very first road trips was to New York after a Saturday night game at home. We got to the hotel and at one or two in the morning, and we had to go through a revolving door to get into the lobby. I had never seen a revolving door before, so instead of letting Ullman walk through on his own I got right in behind him. This was the era of plaid jackets and high platform footwear and I'd brought only one pair of shoes for the entire trip. The heel came off one of my shoes and jammed the door from moving, and Normie and I got stuck. Our suitcases started hitting us and Ullman thought I was being some sort of wise guy. Someone had to be called to get the heel out of the door and set us free, and the next day I had to go shopping in New York to buy another pair of shoes! Norm saw the humour in it all later, but for a while there, early on a Sunday morning in Manhattan, neither of us knew what was going on. Later on, Norm and I did some commercials for Weetabix breakfast cereal that were pretty funny.

◀ **Norm Ullman watches as I fly into the Washington Capitals net after scoring a goal. When I became the first Maple Leafs player to record 100 points in a season, it was Norm Ullman's 85-point mark (set in 1970–71) that was broken (top); Norm Ullman and I plead our case to referee Ron Wicks (bottom).**

JACQUES PLANTE

One of my favourite veterans when I joined the Maple Leafs was goaltender Jacques Plante. Some people may have found Plante a little prickly, but it should be remembered that he came from Montreal, where he was used to winning Stanley Cups. He came to the Leafs at the age of 40 to give the team some veteran experience in goal. He was named to the NHL's second all-star team after the 1970–71 season with Toronto. Plante was also very helpful in the development of Bernie Parent, a goalie we picked up in a deal with Philadelphia in January 1971.

I liked Plante. When he wasn't playing, he would give me helpful hints on what to do. For example, he would suggest I find better shooting angles by coming in off the wing instead of just firing the puck at any opportunity. Off the ice he would play cribbage with me on plane rides. I loved playing the game; it reminded me of being a kid at the cottage. One time while I was playing with Plante I scored a 29 score – in cribbage, it's almost impossible to get 29. I wish I had gotten Jacques to sign those cards as a memory of such a rare event, and so that I would have the autograph of one of the very best Hall of Fame goalies in NHL history.

◀ Jacques Plante in net for the Maple Leafs.
Jacques Plante and I, along with the rest of the team, celebrate a win over the Buffalo Sabres. ▶

DAVE KEON

Dave Keon was the Toronto captain when I joined the team in 1970 and he was one of the greatest Maple Leafs ever. He set an NHL record in 1970–71 when he scored eight shorthanded goals (since broken) and I remember him most for his intensity. He could be abrupt at times but that did not take away from him being a tremendous player. It also did not affect his great work ethic, which rubbed off on me that first year especially.

It was my wish and Toronto management's hope that Keon would at some point officially return to the Leafs. I had talked to Dave about his thoughts on being honoured by the team, such as the time we did the captains photo shoot together. His many fans wanted to see him added to Legends Row or perhaps see a banner in his honour up in the rafters at the Air Canada Centre. In January of 2016 Keon accepted the honour of being put on Legends Row after team president Brendan Shanahan reached out to him and let Keon know he had been nominated. It will be great to see Keon's statue be unveiled in the fall of '16.

It might be another bit of time before we see a Keon banner inside the ACC. It is clear that he does not like the fact that the Maple Leafs do not retire sweater numbers once a banner is raised in honour of a player. The Leafs might have to pay more attention to who gets a particular number more than they have in the past. It should become a priority because at certain times who gets special numbers has gone off the track a little.

I was always honoured to get all the recognition the Maple Leafs have given me over the years. I think if the organization chooses to honour you in a certain manner, then that is the choice of those in charge and I accept it. However if someone says the Leafs should do it like the Canadiens have done it (by retiring sweater numbers), then I can understand that point of view as well.

◀ Dave Keon (when he was captain of the Maple Leafs versus the Pittsburgh Penguins and number 26, Syl Apps Jr.) once held the Toronto team record for most points (858) and goals (396) (top); That is me on the left with Lanny McDonald in the middle and Dave Keon on the right during a Hockey Hall of Fame function (bottom).

CHRISTMAS DAY 1970 AND 1971

December 25, 1970. It was my rookie season, and we had a night game against the Minnesota North Stars. Because we had to play, the day didn't seem very special, so it was nice to receive a telegram from my mom wishing me a Merry Christmas. Unfortunately, we lost the game 6–3. The only good thing that happened that night was teammate Norm Ullman scoring his 400th career goal against Gump Worsley. Interestingly, the North Stars drew 15,199 fans to the game – the second-highest attendance total for a Minnesota home game since they'd entered the league in 1967.

The next year we played at home on December 25. This time we beat the Detroit Red Wings 5–3. Billy MacMillan scored three goals, and Dave Keon was given a minor penalty for slashing in the third period – one of the very few he received throughout his illustrious career. I scored the fifth Leaf goal of the night in the third period when I took a shot that beat Detroit goalie Joe Daley. The assists went to Guy Trottier and Don Marshall. Turns out it was the final Leafs goal scored on a Christmas Day; the NHL hasn't scheduled December 25 games since. That night, 16,485 fans were at Maple Leaf Gardens, many of them youngsters in attendance for "Young Canada Night." Season ticket holders were either given an extra ticket or encouraged to give their seats to young fans who would love the chance to see a Maple Leafs game during the holiday season. It was a great tradition, but it eventually ended when ticket prices got higher and higher.

◀ Bill MacMillan   A telegram from my mom: December 25, 1970. ▶

Telegram

1256P CST DEC 25 70 MA 243 FDA 080

CN TNC513 CNT ZETN STJACOBS ONT 25 148P EST
DARRYL SITTLER   TORONTO MAPLE LEAFS
   METROPOLITAN SPORTS CENTER 7901 CEDAR AVE BLOOMINGTON MINN
MERRY CHRISTMAS TO YOU AND LEAFS KEEP UP THE GOOD WORK LOVE
   MOM DAD AND KIDS
(54).

SF-1201 (R5-69)

JIM MCKENNY

I've always liked Jim "Howie" McKenny. He's a funny guy to be around, but what some people may not realize is that he's also a great human being. He was always a hard worker, very dedicated to the Maple Leafs, and a good teammate. His troubles with addictions have been well documented but he overcame those problems and turned his life around. Everyone still has a great McKenny story, like this one:

We were not allowed to bring beer onto the team bus even though management would often look the other way. One time, McKenny filled a garbage bin with ice and beer and left it in the dressing room so that we could have a few cold ones after the game. He put a garbage bag on top of it all to hide the stash of beer but Johnny McLellan ruined the plan. The normally quiet coach was really mad at us for a period we had just played against Vancouver. He kicked the garbage bin across the room and the beer bottles spilled out all over the dressing room floor! Everyone was looking at Howie, who had a sheepish look on his face.

"HALF THIS GAME IS MENTAL, THE OTHER HALF IS BEING MENTAL." Jim McKenny

---

Jim was always a guy who liked to help people. Today he works in Port Perry, Ontario, helping others overcome their addictions.

I went to the 1988 Goofy Games at Disney World in Florida with Jim when he was a broadcaster at CityTV. We were trying to win money for the Special Olympics by competing against other broadcasters and athletes, such as the National Football League's Boomer Esiason and Bruce Smith.

◀ Jim McKenny and I versus Pittsburgh's Denis Herron in goal and defenseman
Colin Campbell (top); Jim and I dressed up for the "Journey to Norway"
portion of the Goofy Games (bottom).

PAUL HENDERSON

On September 28, 1972, the Maple Leafs were in for a pre-season game against the Canucks. We'd all been caught up in the emotion of the eight-game Summit Series between Canada and Russia, and that afternoon, we gathered together to watch the final game. To us, it seemed like a battle between democracy and communism, and we had to win. It was great to see our teammate Paul Henderson score the winning goal with 34 seconds left to play.

Wendy and I had moved into the Henderson house in Mississauga, Ontario, so we could look after Paul and Eleanor's three daughters while Paul was in Moscow making hockey history. After Paul scored the winner, Wendy and the three very young girls – Heather, Jennifer, and Jill – had to deal with the fame right away. People were coming to the door and asking for pictures. Finally, they had to put a sign up saying they had none left!

Henderson was a very competitive player who loved to score goals. He was incredibly fast and had a good shot. We became friends and often socialized along with the families of Ron Ellis, Brian Glennie, and Tim Ecclestone.

When I scored in overtime to clinch the Canada Cup in '76 it made for some nice symmetry: a Toronto Maple Leaf had scored the winning goal for Canada in two significant international hockey events. Right after the Summit Series was over, Toronto owner Harold Ballard had the switchboard staff at Maple Leaf Gardens answer the phones by saying, "Home of Paul Henderson." He did the same for me in 1976 when the receptionist would answer, "Maple Leaf Gardens, home of Darryl Sittler." It was a nice touch.

With Paul Henderson when he returned to Leaf practice after the 1972 Canada–Russia series. ▶

RON ELLIS

I knew all about Ron Ellis from watching him play for the Maple Leafs on *Hockey Night in Canada*. He was one of the NHL's great up-and-down wingers, a Stanley Cup winner, and a member of Team Canada in 1972. He's the kind of man you would want your son to be; he is such a good person.

"I WOULD HAVE BEEN HONOURED TO BE CAPTAIN OF THE TORONTO MAPLE LEAFS. I COULD HAVE TAKEN IT WHEN IT WAS OFFERED BUT I WAS SO UNCERTAIN OF MY FUTURE AND MY HEALTH. THE FRONT OFFICE MADE THE RIGHT DECISION IN CHOOSING DARRYL AND I WAS WISE NOT TO CAUSE A PROBLEM. DARRYL WAS READY TO BE THE OFFICIAL LEADER." **Ron Ellis**

After Dave Keon left the team at the end of the 1974–75 season, Jim Gregory went to Ellis and asked him about the team captaincy. It was important to speak to Ron about it since he had seniority and the respect of everyone on the team. But instead of taking the position himself, he said I should be named captain. That gave me great confidence, and I was honoured that Ron thought so much of me that he would put my name forward. I was given the C to start the 1975–76 season – a year that saw Ron step away from the game to deal with some personal issues. Luckily for the Leafs, he came back in 1977–78, scoring 26 goals in the regular season and helping us beat the New York Islanders in the playoffs.

◀ Ron Ellis beat Montreal netminder Ken Dryden with just three seconds to play during a contest on March 12, 1975, at Maple Leaf Gardens. I took the faceoff against Peter Mahovlich and got the puck over to Bob Neely before Ron picked up a rebound and tied the game 3–3.

BIGGEST FIGHT

Standing up for yourself on the ice was something I always believed in, even when it included fighting. I prepared myself for on-ice battles by working out with a punching bag, much like boxers do. I wasn't trying to be a great fighter but I wanted to know I could handle myself during the inevitable scraps that were going to come up from time to time. My most celebrated fight came against Garry Howatt of the New York Islanders. He was not the biggest player in the league (five foot nine, 175 pounds) but he could fight.

On March 14, 1973, we went at it during a game at Maple Leaf Gardens. We were up 2–1 in the third period when the fight broke out and Islander coach Al Arbour said to Howatt, "Take him off." Obviously, they wanted me out of the game for five minutes. Howatt, who was in his first full NHL season, got really worked up and grabbed my hair before trying to land a coco butt. We slugged it out until we both fell to our knees, totally exhausted. I'd never felt so tired! Luckily, there were only about four minutes to go when I got out of the penalty box and we hung on for the win. After the game Howatt said, "He's a pretty good guy to take out of the game." It was certainly my most memorable fight, although few people actually saw it. It happened on a Thursday night, when there was no TV broadcast.

During my third season in the NHL, in 1972–73, I had a different sort of "Gordie Howe hat trick" (otherwise known as a goal, an assist, and a fight). During a road game against the Canucks on December 5, I took on Vancouver captain Orland Kurtenbach in a fight and held my own. Kurtenbach (six foot two, 180 pounds) was known as one of the best heavyweight fighters in the NHL, although I had no idea about his reputation at the time. I stood toe to toe with him and did not get beat. Later in that same game, I had another fight, this time against Bobby Schmautz – another pretty good fighter. I did all right in that battle too. I also scored a goal in the game and we won 5–2. I did not register an assist, but I did have two fights and a goal!

The hard-slugging fight between me and Garry Howatt at Maple Leaf Gardens. ▶

THE TORONTO TOROS COME CALLING

By the end of my third season I was earning $29,000, my contract was up, and I had just finished as the Maple Leafs' leading scorer with 77 points. Johnny F. Bassett had just moved the Ottawa Nationals of the WHA to Toronto and renamed them the Toros. After the 1972–73 season, Bassett acquired my WHA rights in a deal with Edmonton and then invited Wendy and me to a dinner at his very posh home in an area of Toronto known as the Bridle Path. I was just 22 at the time and was in awe. I recall seeing Bassett's daughter Carling, who would go on to fame in tennis; she was about five at the time. There were other prominent Toronto businesspeople in attendance, like developer Rudy Bratty and McDonald's Restaurants CEO George Cohon.

When dinner was over Johnny F. got right down to business. What would it take to get Darryl Sittler to become a Toro? he asked my agent. A million for five years (plus other inducements), Alan Eagleson replied. Bassett quickly agreed, but there was a catch: I had to agree to the deal right then and there or it was off the table. For a young guy making just $29,000 a year, this was unbelievable! Somehow, Wendy and I restrained ourselves and I did not take the deal.

I wanted to stay in the NHL and be a Maple Leaf. I got a total package of about $800,000 over five years from the Maple Leafs after Jim Gregory went to see Harold Ballard, who was in jail as a result of his tax evasion conviction. Ballard gave his approval and we scheduled a July media conference to announce the deal.

When I got to the press conference, who should be there but Harold himself, out on a pass and looking fatter than ever. I know Harold wasn't a hardened criminal, and he certainly didn't look like one that day. He was tanned and wearing a checkered shirt. Before we met the press, Harold showed me pictures of himself dressed as a guard while in prison – feet up, watching colour television, smoking a cigar, and drinking beer! This is life in a Canadian prison, he told me. During the news conference, he shared many of these same details with the media. Naturally, there was a major issue made of it, and I am sure some people got into trouble – or at least had some explaining to do!

◀ With Harold Ballard, signing my new Leafs contract.

FOUR

THE CAPTAIN LEADS

THE CAPTAINCY
AND GEORGE ARMSTRONG

George Armstrong was my teammate for the last season of his great career. In fact, he was often the right winger on the line with me and Jim Harrison. Even though he played in only 59 games in 1970–71, he recorded 24 points. "Chief" was no longer captain by the time I joined the team but he had worn the C on his sweater from 1957 to 1969, and won four Stanley Cups. Armstrong was a very humble man, a real character, and a funny guy off the ice. He finished his career as the Leafs' all-time points leader with 713; only four other players have recorded more points since that time with Toronto. He holds many other team records, including most career games played with 1,187 appearances in a Leafs uniform.

It was a real honour when he gave me my first sweater after I was named team captain on September 10, 1975. I was the second-youngest captain in team history and I vowed to be the best captain possible, following the great Leafs tradition set by the likes of Charlie Conacher, Hap Day, Syl Apps, Ted Kennedy, Bob Davidson, Armstrong, and Dave Keon.

I was honoured to be named team captain, and I took the role without any hesitation because I knew I had a great support system in place. Teammates like Dave Williams, Pat Boutette, Borje Salming, and Lanny McDonald were all part of a leadership group that made the job so much easier.

◀ It was pretty cool to get my new sweater with the C stitched on from George Armstrong.

Celebrating a goal with Lanny McDonald. Lanny was a second team all-star on right wing for the 1976–77 season.

LANNY MCDONALD

Lanny McDonald came to training camp in 1973 as a high-priced guy drafted fourth overall by the Leafs. The World Hockey Association was signing a lot of NHL guys away, and Toronto could not afford to lose any more players to the rival league. Lanny went through some growing pains in his first two years, but his work ethic would eventually turn him into one of the best right wingers in the NHL.

Coach Red Kelly put Lanny and me on the same line in 1975–76, and it soon became an instinctive and intuitive situation. Each of us knew where the other was going on the ice. Lanny came to play every night, and he had a great, very accurate shot. He scored 37 times in the 1975–76 season and then added 46 the following year (the fifth-best mark in the league). He notched 47 in 1977–78, recording the fourth-highest total that year.

During the 1977 playoffs, in a game against Pittsburgh, I gave Lanny a pass to put into an empty net. I could have scored the goal myself, but how many chances do you get to score three goals in one playoff game? I felt I had to pass Lanny the puck and see him record the hat trick. Later on during the 1977 playoffs versus Philadelphia, Lanny scored four goals in one game.

Off the ice Lanny and I became best friends, as did our wives, Wendy and Ardell. After Wendy passed away, Ardell played an instrumental role in the lives of my daughters, Meaghan and Ashley, and was very helpful to them. Ardell not only gave the eulogy at Wendy's funeral, she was also asked to speak when the girls got married. My friendship with Lanny is one that lasts to this day.

"LANNY MCDONALD IS A TRULY GENUINE GUY, DOWN-TO-EARTH, SINCERE, A CHARACTER WITH A BIG HEART. THE GREAT LOVE HE HAS FOR HIS WIFE AND KIDS HAS TO BE SEEN TO BE BELIEVED. HE'S A ONE-OF-A-KIND TYPE OF GUY AND HAS THE DEPENDABILITY AND GENEROSITY INSIDE THAT MAKES HIM A FRIEND FOR LIFE." **Darryl Sittler**

ERROL THOMPSON

Errol Thompson was drafted in the same year I was, 1970, going 22nd overall to the Maple Leafs. It took Thompson a couple of years to become a regular player on the team, and he worked hard to graduate from the "Black Aces" – the guys who practised every day but were not always sure they were going to play. By the 1974–75 season, his hard work paid off; he had 25 goals and 42 points in 65 games.

The next year saw Errol play alongside Lanny and me for most of the season. He responded with a career-best 43 goals (the top mark on the team) and 80 points. That 1975–76 season saw our line become one of the best in the entire league, and the three of us totalled 161 goals and 273 points. Thompson was perhaps a little bit underrated; he had good speed and a good shot and that made him dangerous on the attack. Our line was fully intact the night I recorded 10 points against Boston – and Thompson and McDonald were a key part of the reason I had such a big night.

Thompson was unhappy to leave Toronto when he was included in the deal that saw Dan Maloney come to the Maple Leafs, but he went on to score 34 for the Red Wings in 1979–80. He totalled 393 points (including 208 goals) in 599 career games.

Thompson in action with the Maple Leafs during the ten-point night versus Boston (top); ▶ McDonald, me, and Thompson looking over fan mail during the height of our popularity as one of the best lines in the NHL (bottom).

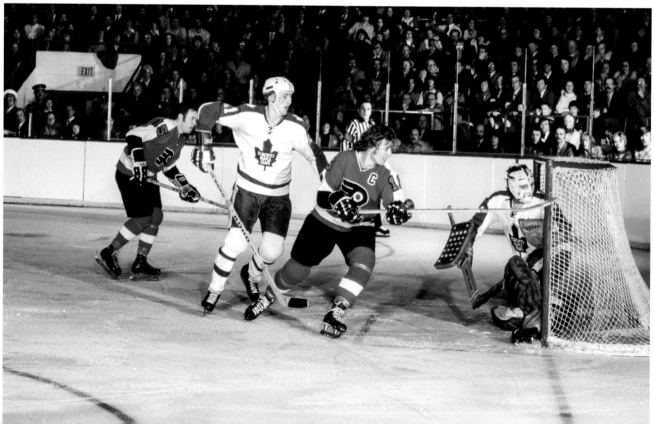

BORJE SALMING

Borje Salming was a highly competitive, all-star-calibre defenceman from the moment he joined the Maple Leafs in 1973–74. He was a pure athlete without an ounce of fat on him. He had an extraordinary mental toughness that never allowed intimidation to take him off his game. Salming played at a time when Swedes and other European players were still thought of as being afraid, or called "chicken Swede" if you got physical with them.

The Flyers certainly tried that approach with Borje. One time, during the 1976 playoffs, he was caught out on the ice without much help, and Flyer Mel Bridgman delivered a serious beating during an all-out brawl. The very next game saw Borje score a great goal on Bernie Parent after I hit him with a pass at centre ice. The crowd at the Gardens erupted in cheers.

The Maple Leaf power play was one of the best in the NHL when Salming manned the point along with Ian Turnbull. Both defencemen had great shots from the blue line, making it doubly tough for the opposition to defend. If Salming had been on one of the Stanley Cup teams of the era, I believe he would have won a Norris Trophy. As it was he finished second for the award on two occasions (and in the top five seven times) and was a six-time league all-star.

"DARRYL SITTLER HIT ME WITH A PERFECT BREAKAWAY PASS AND I SCORED ON GOALIE BERNIE PARENT. SOMEHOW IT FELT AS IF I HAD SHOWN MEL BRIDGMAN. IT IS ONE OF THE FEW GOALS I REMEMBER CLEARLY, PARTLY BECAUSE OF THE STANDING OVATION I RECEIVED FROM THE WONDERFUL TORONTO SUPPORTERS." **Borje Salming**

◀ Borje Salming and I attack at the Montreal net (top);
Salming (shown here against Bobby Clarke) holds the Maple Leafs
record for most career assists, with 620 (bottom).

IAN TURNBULL

Ian Turnbull was a different kind of guy. I sat beside him in the Maple Leafs dressing room all those years, and was never quite sure what I was going to get. Sometimes, he could be a little aloof, casual, and moody. I don't know if Ian ever reached his potential, but during the 1978 playoff series against the New York Islanders, he rose to the occasion when Borje Salming got hurt in the fourth game. Turnbull had played in Salming's shadow since they'd both joined the team in 1973–74, but Ian played his best hockey in that series. In the seventh game, he scored the goal that tied us 1–1, and then made the pass that sprung Lanny McDonald loose for the series winner.

Maybe Ian was used to being cast behind star defencemen – he'd played junior with Denis Potvin in Ottawa. I believe he could have reached his true talent level on a team where he was the main guy on the blue line, but he never got that opportunity. One thing for sure was that Turnbull and Salming were terrific together on the Maple Leafs power play. They could both fire the puck from the point. Ian set a team record for defencemen (which still stands) when he had 79 points (22 goals, 57 assists) in 1976–77. He also scored five goals in one game against Detroit on February 2, 1977 – another mark he holds for Toronto defencemen, though it established the NHL record for blue liners as well.

◀ **Ian Turnbull up the ice versus the Rangers, with me behind him.**

MIKE PALMATEER

The Maple Leafs drafted goalie Mike Palmateer in 1974, and by the early stages of the 1976–77 season, he had become the team's number one goalie. He was a very colourful player, with a confident and cocky style on the ice. He was also a bit of a showman, and could make a routine save look difficult. Those types of saves would get into the opposition's head, especially when the Gardens crowd responded to his acrobatic style. They might come down the ice on the next rush and try to beat Palmateer with a high shot aimed at his head, just to get back at him, but he never hesitated to come out and challenge the shooter right up close. He made a lot of great saves when he was hot, which worked to our advantage and got us going as well.

Palmy was at his best against the New York Islanders in the 1978 playoffs, and he made two saves that really stood out for us in the 2–1 overtime win. The first came in regulation play. He got caught behind the net and it looked like Bryan Trottier was going to score with ease. Somehow, Mike dove back in front of the net and got his stick on Trottier's drive to deflect it. Then, early in the overtime session, he stopped Billy Harris on a great opportunity before Lanny scored the winner for us.

Mike was great for us again in the 1979 post-season, when we beat Atlanta and gave Montreal a good battle. However, the Leafs (managed at this point by Punch Imlach and Harold Ballard) were worried about his knee problems and refused to sign him to a new deal. One of the top goalies in the league was dealt to the Washington Capitals in June of 1980. He returned to the Maple Leafs for two final years starting in 1982.

RED KELLY

Red Kelly was my second coach when I played for the Maple Leafs. He took over from Johnny McLellan starting with the 1973–74 season. At that time, the team was made up of many new faces plus some veterans. Red was respected as a Hall of Famer who had played the game at a very high level. Red was a real gentleman; he never swore, preferring to use words like *hang* or *dang* when he was upset. I liked Red, but he was an old-school guy who just ran drills in practice. We made the playoffs every year under Red but could not get past Boston or Philadelphia.

In the '76 playoffs Kelly decided we would benefit from "Pyramid Power," something his teenage daughter was using to help ward off migraine headaches. She had studied the effects of the pyramids and learned that this geometrical form had some hidden mystic power or psychic energy. The Flyers had singer Kate Smith singing "God Bless America" as a good luck charm before their home games, so I guess Red thought we had to counter.

I wasn't convinced about "Pyramid Power," but Red was! He had pyramids placed under the benches in our dressing room and under the team bench as well. I don't know if there was any real effect, but that was the night I scored five goals in one playoff game. For our next game in Philadelphia we had a big pyramid in the middle of the dressing room. We all took turns sitting under it in preparation for the seventh and deciding contest of the series. Even though I still wasn't certain about all this, I was not about to tempt fate after a five-goal night. We were up 2–1 after the first period but we ended up on the wrong end of a 7–3 final. In 1977 we also lost to Philadelphia in the playoffs and that ended Red Kelly's time as coach of the Maple Leafs.

◀ **With Red Kelly at the Leafs bench.**

DAVE "TIGER" WILLIAMS

The first time I saw Dave "Tiger" Williams was at a Leafs training camp in 1974, and he made quite a first impression. I was the first one on the ice on the opening day of camp and was skating around very casually, shooting a puck off the boards or into the empty net. Before he got on the ice, I could see him standing by the gate at the bench. He was taking it all in, as he looked around Maple Leaf Gardens, appreciating the moment of making it all the way to the NHL. We had heard about how tough he was (854 career penalty minutes in three years for the Swift Current Broncos) but he could also score (44- and 52-goal seasons in his last two years of junior). Tiger got on and skated the length of the ice before leaping up and crashing into the glass above the boards at the end of the rink. He did it again at the other end of the ice. Later that day he fought Ian Turnbull, who had to use his great strength to subdue the feisty Tiger. He didn't make the team out of camp, but our second-round draft choice returned in the middle of the 1974–75 season and never looked back. Tiger became our enforcer, and he showed how much he loved that role by taking on the NHL's toughest customers on his way to 3,966 career penalty minutes!

Tiger was in great condition and very intense about everything he did. That approach kept other players honest – including his teammates. If Tiger thought one of us was floating, you can bet he let us know. Williams thrived under coach Roger Neilson, and when Roger was let go late in the 1978–79 season, it was Tiger who spoke up, suggesting that the players should ask upper management to keep the coach around. Tiger asked me to speak to Jim Gregory about letting Roger stay. Eventually, Harold Ballard agreed.

Williams was very disappointed to be traded to Vancouver in 1980, and when he came back to the Gardens on the night of December 10, 1980, he made it a game to remember. Tiger scored to give Vancouver a 5–4 lead in the third period and then rode his stick all the way down the ice! When he was with the Maple Leafs, Williams used to touch the tigers Ballard had had painted at centre ice (to remind Toronto fans that he also owned the CFL's Hamilton Tiger-Cats). I saw what he was doing but I wasn't mad at him – it was Tiger being Tiger. He had been a great teammate and to this day he is still my great friend.

I still like to kid Tiger about the fact that he was a minus-two the night I recorded 10 points against the Boston Bruins. We scored 11 goals in total that night, and Boston only got four, but Tiger still managed to come out a minus-two. Amazing!

DAVE REECE

Boston goalie Dave Reece has always been a pretty good sport about his part in my 10-point night. While it's true he didn't play in the NHL again after that game on February 7, 1976, he does have a winning record for his 14 NHL appearances – going 7–5–2 with two shutouts during the 1975–76 season (the Leafs and Bruins played three games prior to the February 7 contest, but he was the backup and never saw a minute of action against us). Boston had originally signed him as a free agent in 1972. His good play in the minors earned him a backup role to Gilles Gilbert to start the 1975–76 season, and once the game at the Gardens was over, the former University of Vermont goalie returned to the American Hockey League (AHL) for the balance of his career.

A native of Troy, New York, Reece also played for the United States at the World Hockey Championships in 1977. After his retirement at the age of 28, Reece moved into the education field. We had not spoken after the 10-point night until TSN brought us together for a 30th anniversary look back at the game. He was very gracious reminiscing about what had gone on back in '76. I think he also showed a great sense of humour when he named his dog Sittler!

"IT JUST WASN'T MY NIGHT AND DARRYL WAS PURE MAGIC. THE LEAFS WERE GOING NUTS, BUT I NEVER REALIZED HE WAS DOING ALL THE SCORING OR GOING FOR A RECORD. THAT'S THE FUN OF SPORTS, BUT SOMETIMES I WONDER WHY I WASN'T PULLED AFTER FIVE OR SIX GOALS."

Goaltender Dave Reece on Darryl Sittler's 10-point game

Celebrating the 40th anniversary of my 10-point night, with Dave Reece and my former teammates. ▶

TEA SERVICE

In appreciation of my 10-point night, Maple Leafs owner Harold Ballard wanted to give me a gift. Before our home playoff game against Pittsburgh on April 9, 1976, Ballard presented my family with a silver tea service, valued at $8,500. He chose something he thought would last for many years, rather than an item that would eventually wear out, like a car or a boat. Many years ago now, I had it appraised for insurance purposes; it was valued at $35,000 – more than four times the original value.

I still have the tea service today, and although its net worth goes up and down with the price of silver, its true value is in the gesture made by Mr. Ballard.

◀ **Clarence Campbell presents me, Wendy, and Ryan with a silver tea service in honour of my 10-point night.**

1976 CANADA CUP WITH THE ROCKET

After every Canada Cup match-up, a player-of-the-game award was handed out to a participant deemed worthy for his efforts in that particular contest. I received the award on September 15, 1976 – the night I scored the tournament-clinching goal. I received an Inuit carving of a bird from Maurice "Rocket" Richard. It was a thrill for me to meet the legendary Hall of Famer.

Just after I received the award, the team got caught up in the emotion of the moment and started exchanging sweaters with the Czech players. I got number 25 from Bohuslav Ebermann, and he got my number 27. I have no idea where that jersey may have ended up! I often think it would be nice to have that sweater, but I do still have the stick and gloves I used when I scored the winning goal in overtime. I gave Ebermann's sweater to the Hockey Hall of Fame.

Wearing Czech sweater number 25 (third from the right) after the exchange (top); ▶
Maurice Richard comes out to present me with the player-of-the-game award, September 15, 1976 (bottom).

27
76 Canada Cup

D.BALL '76

AN INVITE FROM THE TRUDEAUS

After we won the first Canada Cup tournament in 1976, Team Canada was invited to 24 Sussex Drive in Ottawa to meet the Prime Minister. We had a cocktail reception at the Prime Minister's house and the Trudeau kids were in their pyjamas – Justin, the oldest son who was about five at the time, was there along with his two younger brothers. We then went to another location for a reception with more than a thousand dignitaries and invitees.

Team captain Bobby Clarke could not attend so I was asked to speak on behalf of the team. I was pretty young at the time, and yet there I was, sitting with my wife, Wendy, and the PM and his wife, Margaret. Senator Keith Davey asked me what I was thinking about saying in my speech to the crowd, and he wisely suggested I talk about the team coming together from all parts of Canada. This was just after the Parti Québécois won the provincial election in Quebec, making national unity a very sensitive subject. I pointed out how English and French players had come together to win the Canada Cup and that the country could do the same and work together. It turned out to be a good idea because I got a standing ovation!

It is interesting to note that nearly 40 years later, young Justin Trudeau is now the prime minister of Canada! I wonder if he remembers the visit Team Canada made to his house back in 1976?

◀ Wendy and me with Prime Minister Trudeau and his wife, Margaret.

A program of the evening's events, signed by the Trudeaus, ▶ and the notes for my speech. My name is the only one that is misspelled in the entire listing of players – Deryl!

TEAM CANADA 1976
L'EQUIPE CANADA 1976

Players — Joueurs		
Bill Barber	Guy Lafleur	Rene Robert
Dan Bouchard	Guy Lapointe	Glenn Resch
Dave Burrows	Reg Leach	Larry Robinson
Gerry Cheevers	Peter Mahovlich	Serge Savard
Bobby Clarke	Dan Maloney	Steve Shutt
Marcel Dionne	Richard Martin	Paul Shmyr
Phil Esposito	Lanny McDonald	Deryl Sittler
Bob Gainey	Bobby Orr	Rogatien Vachon
Danny Gare	Gilbert Perrault	Carol Vadnais
Bobby Hull	Denis Potvin	Jim Watson
	Jean Pronovost	

Coaches — Instructeurs	Trainers — Entraîneurs
Scotty Bowman	Ed Palchak
"Toe" Blake	Lefty Wilson
Al MacNeil	
Don Cherry	**Team Doctor — Médecin**
Bob Kromm	Dr. Doug Kinnear

Managing Director — Directeur-gérant
Sam Pollock

Business Management — Administration

Keith Allen	Bill Watters
Mike Cannon	William Sutton
Lee Dillon	

Canada Cup of Hockey Organizing Committee — Comité d'organisation du tournoi de hockey de la coupe Canada

Alan Eagleson	Don Johnson
Doug Fisher	Paul Woodstock
Derek Holmes	

ROGER NEILSON

Roger Neilson took over as coach of the Maple Leafs in 1977 after Red Kelly was let go. Roger brought a fresh approach, including accountability on the ice, and the use of statistics to prepare us for games and to improve our off-ice conditioning programs. He was a forward-thinking guy with plenty of good innovations. He made every one of us feel important, which made life better for me as a player and captain. Under his leadership, there was a sense that we were all in it together, and that made for a tightly knit team. At that time, the team had a lot of "character" guys. Roger made sure we were included in the decision-making process. We also knew that he cared about us as people, and was concerned about what was going on in our lives besides hockey.

Roger left nothing to chance. He gave us structure for everything so we would always be prepared. He wanted no excuses for losing. We were going to be physical and finish every check. He had us ready to go through the man if we had to, and that made us difficult to play against. We didn't play a "firewagon" style of game, but we tried not to beat ourselves. Roger was all about matchups and strategies. He was a real thinker and studied the game closely. He coached eight NHL teams throughout his career.

I had my best years with Roger behind the Leafs bench. I think I was truly ready for his approach to the game. The coaches who followed him as the Leafs' bench boss while I was there were never quite as good. Roger was elected to the Hockey Hall of Fame in 2002.

"HE'S A GREAT COACH, A MAN WITH A LOT OF PRIDE IN COACHING AND A TREMENDOUS WORKER. I HAD MY BEST YEAR IN HOCKEY LAST YEAR AND HE HAD A LOT TO DO WITH IT." **Darryl Sittler on Roger Neilson, March 1, 1979**

Me, Roger Neilson, and Lanny McDonald, on the cover of the *Toronto Star*'s television magazine. ▶

Star Week

TV listings and entertainment guide

October 15 to 22, 1977

TORONTO

Leafs' Sittler, Neilson and McDonald - new goals for a new season

Lanny McDonald beats Glenn "Chico" Resch with the overtime winner in game seven.

BEATING THE NEW YORK ISLANDERS

Three straight playoff losses to the Philadelphia Flyers in 1975, 1976, and 1977 made us hungry for a playoff win in a seven-game series. In 1978 we beat the Los Angeles Kings in two straight but came up against a very good New York Islanders team in the quarter-finals. We had a team meeting with coach Roger Neilson before the series, and it was clear that we all believed we could win the series, although we knew it wasn't going to be easy. We lost the first two games in New York (one in overtime), but we kept believing in ourselves. Roger had prepared us for this all season long, and we came back to win the series on Lanny McDonald's overtime goal in game seven. Although we did get a good break when the puck bounced to Lanny in the clear, winning this series was no fluke.

As we mobbed each other on the ice we started to sing Queen's "We Are the Champions," which was the Islanders' song that year. They played it all the time, but we decided to enjoy the lyrics ourselves when the series was over. It was sweet to win the series on Long Island, especially after we'd dropped a couple of games there in overtime (on goals by Mike Bossy and Bob Nystrom). It marked the first time the Maple Leafs had won a seven-game series since their Stanley Cup win in 1967.

Lanny jumps on me to start the celebration of our victory ▶ over the New York Islanders in seven hard-fought games.

CELEBRATING WITH THE FANS

After beating the Islanders in the 1978 quarter-final series, we arrived back at the Toronto airport early on a Sunday morning. Even so, there were plenty of fans to greet us. It was great to see them come out to show their support. I think the 1977–78 team captured the imagination of so many Torontonians. We had a colourful, close-knit group of guys with great character. The fans seemed to appreciate our efforts, and the fact that we had finally won a major playoff series.

The guys were invited back to my house in Mississauga for a little celebration. Some fans decided to follow us home. One of them was a 19-year-old named Dave Poulin. He and his buddies were looking over the fence into my backyard when Dan Maloney spotted them. Maloney could be a pretty intimidating guy and he shooed them away. Poulin was born in Timmins, Ontario, but moved to Mississauga when he was eight and played minor hockey in the Toronto area.

In March 1983, Poulin became my teammate when he signed with Philadelphia. On April 2 of that year, I recorded an assist on Poulin's first NHL goal – against Mike Palmateer in a 6–3 Flyers win over Toronto at the Gardens. Poulin scored another goal in that game (his only two of the season) and I got my 42nd of the year, so it was a memorable night.

◀ Mobbed by Leafs fans who came out to greet us at the airport
after we'd beaten the Islanders in the 1978 playoffs.
I recorded an assist on Dave Poulin's first NHL goal. ▶

FIVE

GREAT OPPONENTS

BRYAN TROTTIER

Bryan Trottier was the best all-round forward during my time in the NHL. He could do just about anything, and I knew I was in for a battle whenever I went up against the New York Islander centre. Bryan was very solid on his skates, and even though he was not a big man, he could battle in the corners with anyone. He had great balance that allowed him to absorb bodychecks and keep going. He could deliver hits, too, but you never had to worry that he was going to do anything bad. Trottier could score goals and was an excellent set-up man for talented wingers like Mike Bossy and Clark Gillies. The entire line made it to the Hockey Hall of Fame.

BOBBY ORR

Bobby Orr was simply phenomenal. He was bigger than life out on the ice and could take control of any situation with ease, usually by speeding the game up (or down, if he wanted to). In the early years of my career, until 1974–75, Orr was absolutely the best player in the league. He was unbelievably competitive and was especially dominating at the Boston Garden, with its smaller rink. I recall being his teammate for the 1976 Canada Cup, and how he had to put large icepacks on his knees after every game just to play the next one. Bobby was very quiet and shy, even though he won everything he possibly could have – including the NHL's scoring title, twice, while he played on defence! I got to know Orr off the ice when I attended the Orr-Walton Sports Camp in the summers as an instructor, and I can say he was special in every way.

"... ONE OF THE CLASSIEST GUYS ON THE ICE – DARRYL SITTLER."

Bobby Orr introducing me at the 1980 Conn Smythe Sports Celebrities Dinner in Toronto

One time, after I had set up Lanny for an empty-net goal during a playoff game against the Pittsburgh Penguins, so he could get a hat trick, Bobby called Wendy to say he thought I'd made a very unselfish play. The fact that he took the time to call my wife says everything that needs to be said about him. I appreciated it very much.

Playing baseball with Bobby (left); ▶
Battling Bobby in front of the Bruins' net (right).

GUY LAFLEUR

I loved watching Guy Lafleur play. During my time in the NHL, he was a prolific goal scorer and one of the top players in the league, if not the best, especially after Bobby Orr retired. He had a knack for scoring when it was needed most, which he could do with his terrific shot. Guy was a great skater with tremendous balance and an ability to change pace; you could never corner him for very long, if at all. His excellent skating was a big part of the reason he scored so many goals and racked up the points during his Hall of Fame career.

◀ Guy Lafleur and I pose before an All-Star Game. Lafleur assisted on my very first All-Star Game goal on January 21, 1975, in Montreal. Later in the same game, we both assisted on a Bobby Orr goal in a 7–1 win for our side – the Wales Conference. In the 1980 All-Star Game, we both assisted on a goal by Ron Stackhouse in a 6–3 Wales win at Detroit.

PHIL ESPOSITO

The thing I admired most about Phil Esposito was that he could just score goals. Phil would get in front of the net and shoot the puck in, usually from right in the slot. He was deadly on the power play and he could stay out on the ice for really long shifts – something no coach would allow today. I had a great deal of respect for how he handled tough situations against the Russians in 1972; he let it be known in an outspoken manner what Team Canada needed to do to win that eight-game series. In the end, he and Paul Henderson were named the Canadian MVPs of that historic summit.

Phil was a teammate for the 1976 Canada Cup, and one of our best veteran players with seven points (four goals, three assists) in seven games played. I recall one game against Russia when coach Scotty Bowman put Lanny McDonald and me in as Phil's wingers for a few shifts. It was part of Bowman's strategy to keep the Russians off balance, and it worked – we won the game 3–1 at Maple Leaf Gardens.

With Phil at the Canada Cup. ▶

GREAT GOALIES

I always liked Boston goalie Gerry Cheevers. He was a very colourful guy, always good for a chuckle. He was also a two-time Stanley Cup winner (1970, 1972). Cheevers would come out to challenge you, and he was really good at handling the puck. His skills in this area helped keep the Bruins out of trouble in their own end, so opposing teams knew it was important to keep the puck away from him if at all possible.

Cheevers also had a way of settling his team down. After my 10-point night, the Bruins went home to play Detroit the next night; Gerry shut them out 7–0. He returned from a brief stint in the WHA during that 1975–76 season, and helped the Bruins get back to the Stanley Cup final in 1977 and 1978. He was elected to the Hall of Fame in 1985. Whenever I see Gerry these days, he is still the same good guy.

Bernie Parent joined the Maple Leafs in my rookie year after a three-team trade between Toronto, Boston, and Philadelphia. He played some great hockey for us. You could see right away that Parent was good, and he was learning how to be better by watching Jacques Plante. Unfortunately, Leafs owner Harold Ballard bungled the contract negotiations with Bernie and his agent and we lost the rising-star netminder to the World Hockey Association.

When he left the WHA, Bernie refused to come back to the Maple Leafs and returned instead to Philadelphia. He went to the right place! Once the Flyers put a good team around him they won two straight Stanley Cups with Bernie starring in net.

On April 22, 1976, I took eight shots on Parent and somehow five went in. Bernie rarely gave up five goals in one game – let alone to one player – but that night we managed an 8–5 win at the Gardens to even our '76 playoff series at three games each.

◀ With Cheevers and and Johnny Bower rinkside at the Boston Garden (top);
Versus Parent and the Flyers at Maple Leaf Gardens (bottom).

BOB GAINEY AND DOUG JARVIS

Bob Gainey was a teammate and linemate during the 1976 Canada Cup tournament and I never realized until then what tremendous condition he was in physically. I always prided myself on being in the best shape possible from a conditioning point of view but Bob was simply amazing. You had to respect the way he played and was very willing to be physical but never handed out any cheap shots. He was very competitive, even if it was in a more defensive role on left wing, but he could also score goals. His great two-way game made him very valuable player in Montreal's success during the 1970s and into the 1980s. Gainey and centre Doug Jarvis were the two guys Lanny McDonald and I faced every time we played the Canadiens. It was never an easy night! Gainey was a part of five Stanley Cup teams and was elected to the Hockey Hall of Fame in 1992.

Jarvis was not a big player at five foot nine and 170 pounds but he was excellent on faceoffs and very tenacious in all parts of the ice. He was also a mentally strong player and although he did not have high offensive numbers, Jarvis had a knack for scoring goals at the most opportune moments or setting one up. Jarvis, a native of Brantford, Ontario, was drafted by the Maple Leafs (24th overall in 1975) but never played a game for Toronto before Montreal acquired him in a trade prior to the start of the 1975–76 season. Montreal was looking for a centre who could win faceoffs, and based on the recommendation of his junior coach in Peterborough (Roger Neilson), the Canadiens made a great deal to acquire Jarvis. He would play in 964 consecutive games with Montreal, Washington, and Hartford before he retired.

In this photo Doug Jarvis (#21) is trying to stop me from scoring against Canadiens netminder Ken Dryden. The Montreal Forum was my favourite road arena to play in since it always had a great hockey atmosphere.

Versus Bob Gainey at Maple Leaf Gardens (left); ▶
Jarvis trying to check me during a game at the Montreal Forum (right).

MARCEL DIONNE AND ROGIE VACHON

The Los Angeles Kings had two main stars in the 1970s – goaltender Rogie Vachon and centre Marcel Dionne. I first knew of Dionne from his junior days as a dynamic player for the St. Catharines Blackhawks between 1968 and 1971. He was a very smart player who was very competitive but did not always get the recognition he deserved while playing for the Kings. Marcel was a very consistent player and one of the greatest all-time point-producing players in NHL history (his 1,771 point total ranks him sixth all-time). He used a short stick and learned how to snap a shot off and was especially good in close. His stocky physique made it difficult to knock him off stride.

Marcel helped set up my winning goal in the 1976 Canada Cup with a great cross-ice pass that I was able to take into the Czech end of the ice to score the winner in overtime. Dionne played for Team Canada a total of six times over his Hall of Fame career. I got to know him a little better at the NHLPA meetings and came to know him as a really good person.

Vachon was a small, competitive goalie who knew how to win from his Montreal days with the Canadiens when he helped them to the Stanley Cup in 1968 and 1969. He was the main guy in the '76 Canada Cup, where he stood very tall to record six wins in seven games played while allowing just 10 goals. He was a very hard-working goalie and playing for a defensively oriented team like the Kings was very helpful to him for many years.

He had a harder time when he went to Detroit but finished his career with two winning seasons in Boston. Rogie was also a very classy guy, and I recall one time he sent a cigar to Mike Palmateer in our dressing room after we beat the Kings in a playoff game. It was Rogie's way of telling Mike he had played a great game. From my point of view Vachon and Palmateer were very similar in style and approach.

◀ **Sittler vs. Vachon during a Leafs/Kings game at Maple Leaf Gardens (top); With Marcel Dionne (bottom).**

BOBBY CLARKE

Bobby Clarke was one of the toughest players to go up against. Since we both played centre, we faced each other many times. He joined the NHL a year before I did and was with Team Canada during the 1972 Summit Series, which was a strong indicator of how well he was playing after just three years as a pro. I considered my performances against Clarke as a measurement of where I was at any given time. I always enjoyed the challenge of playing against the best opponents, and Clarke fit the bill: he was league MVP three times, plus a two-time winner of the Stanley Cup.

What I admired most about Clarke was that he was a dedicated competitor who would do anything to win. He was much respected around the entire league and his work ethic was second to none. I got to see this up close when we were teammates on the 1976 Canada Cup team. I felt there was mutual respect between us, even though he captained the Flyers and I captained the Maple Leafs during a time when the teams were great rivals. Clarke was not a big man but he was very tough to move off the puck, so it was always an intense battle facing him. You also had to respect the fact that he did so much despite being a diabetic.

We got along as teammates (we even worked out together) after I was dealt to Philadelphia in 1982, but my feelings about Clarke the man changed when he became the Flyers' general manager. To "Bob" Clarke I was just a tradeable commodity, and at the time, I was naive about how he would treat people. He did make a good hockey deal when he traded me to Detroit, but I thought the truth about being offered the captaincy was just as important. Clarke didn't agree. I lost my respect for him and for the way the business of hockey was conducted.

Keeping a close eye on Clarke during a game at Maple Leaf Gardens (top); ▶
With Clarke and Alan Eagleson at the World Championships (bottom).

LARRY ROBINSON

Larry Robinson always had a presence about him on the ice. He was big (six foot four and 225 pounds), strong, and his hits were hard but clean. Montreal coach Scotty Bowman made sure he was out against my line whenever the Leafs and Canadiens played. Robinson never went looking for trouble, but he never backed away from a scrap, especially if a teammate needed help. Larry was also very good offensively (958 career points) and exceptional at rushing the puck up the ice.

During the 1979 playoffs, I got to witness first-hand what a classy guy Robinson could be. Just after he scored in overtime to eliminate the Leafs, Larry did his best to help control an outraged Tiger Williams, who was sitting in the penalty box when Robinson shot the winner past Paul Harrison into the Leafs net. Tiger was trying to get at a referee (Bob Myers, who made the penalty call), but Robinson told him it wasn't worth it. In his recent book, *The Great Defender: My Hockey Odyssey*, Larry was kind enough to say that the Maple Leafs of 1978 and 1979 were not an easy team to beat, even though the Canadiens won eight straight playoff games against us over those two years!

GORDIE HOWE

My first year in the NHL was Gordie Howe's last with the Detroit Red Wings. Many thought it would be his final season in hockey, but he came back to play in the World Hockey Association in 1973. During that 1970–71 season, though, we played a game in Detroit on November 1. The young Leafs defenceman Mike Pelyk was harassing Howe during the game and I guess Gordie did not take it too well. At one point, as he was falling down, he swung his stick, striking Pelyk right on the mouth and cutting his upper lip pretty badly. Pelyk needed 25 stitches and it was feared he had also suffered a broken jaw. Howe made it look like it was an accident because of his stumble, and because Mike was falling down too, but all of us knew it was Howe implementing his legendary payback!

When Howe returned to the NHL for the 1979–80 season, he appeared in his final All-Star Game. It was an honour to play on the same team as Gordie for this contest, which was held in Detroit at Joe Louis Arena. The Wales Conference beat the Campbell Conference 6–4, and Howe got an assist on the final goal of the game for the winning side. What I remember most, though, was the tremendous ovation Gordie received in the city where he'd dominated for so many years. It was an emotional moment for those of us who were lucky enough to witness this great reception for the soon-to-be 52-year-old legend.

I attended Gordie's funeral in June of 2016 and there were many more stories and memories shared about Howe's long career by everyone in the game, including Wayne Gretzky, Guy Lafleur, and Bobby Orr. It was a privilege for me to be there to honour "Mr. Hockey."

Gordie Howe and Guy Lafleur at the NHL All-Star Game, played in Detroit on February 5, 1980 (left); ▶
Maple Leafs captain Dave Keon presents Gordie Howe with a silver tray
on March 31, 1971, in appreciation of Howe's 43rd birthday and to celebrate his 25 years in
the NHL. The presentation took place on "Gordie Howe Day" in Toronto, and the hockey legend
received many accolades before the game was played that night (right).

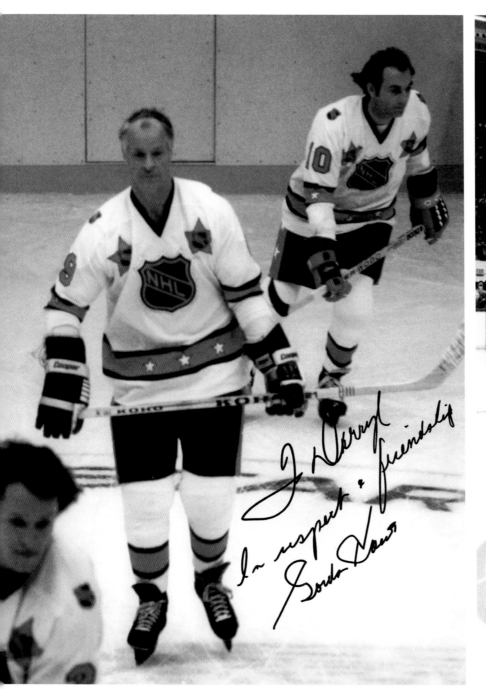

To Darryl
In respect & friendship
Gordie Howe

SIX

MY LAST DAYS AS A MAPLE LEAF

MY 300TH CAREER GOAL AS A MAPLE LEAF

The 1979–80 season was a very difficult one for the Maple Leafs. There were changes in coaching and management, and many of the players who had been with Toronto the previous two seasons were gone (including Jerry Butler, Pat Boutette, Dave Hutchison, Lanny McDonald, Walt McKechnie, and Tiger Williams). For me, one of the few bright spots was scoring my 300th goal in a home game against the Quebec Nordiques on January 5, 1980. Ironically, I got it against a former teammate, Ron Low, who was in net for Quebec. The goal came in the third period, and even though we lost the game 7–3, the crowd gave me a lengthy ovation.

Only four players have ever scored 300 goals in a Maple Leafs uniform: Mats Sundin (420), me (389), Dave Keon (365), and Ron Ellis (332). Three others have scored more than 290: Rick Vaive (299), George Armstrong (296), and Frank Mahovlich (296).

ALL-STAR GAMES AND THE 1979 CHALLENGE CUP

The first All-Star Game I was invited to was in 1974. It was scheduled for Tuesday, January 19, at the Chicago Stadium. On the Sunday night before the game, however, Wendy gave birth to our first child, and I had to get back to London, Ontario, to be with her and our new son, Ryan. Leafs defenceman Jim McKenny, who was in Chicago for NHL Players' Association (NHLPA) meetings, took my spot in the game.

While my family was my first priority, I hated missing that game! I had no idea if I would ever get invited back. As it turned out, I played in the game the very next season, as part of the Wales Conference team that whipped the Campbell Conference squad 7–1 at the Montreal Forum. I scored the third goal of the game to give the Wales a 3–0 lead in the first period with a shot that beat goalie Gary Smith of the Vancouver Canucks. Syl Apps Jr. won the 1975 MVP award. I enjoyed playing in the All-Star Game, and looked forward to it each time I was asked. The gala dinners held the night before the game were great events too, and each player was presented with a gift to commemorate his participation. One year it was a nice watch; I gave it to Wendy and she used it as a necklace.

In 1979 the NHL tried something different. Instead of a conference-against-conference game, the best NHL players took on the Soviet national team in the Challenge Cup – a three-game series held in New York. We were allowed to bring our wives, which made the event even more special, and we stayed at one of the fanciest hotels in New York – the Waldorf-Astoria. The NHL was supposed to win, and we did take the first game 4–2, but the Russians came back to win the next contest 5–4 and then hammered us 6–0 to take the series. Despite the loss it was a rare thrill to compete with and against the era's best hockey players.

◀ Facing the Soviet national team at the Challenge Cup in 1979 (left); At the NHL All-Star Game in Buffalo on January 24, 1978, shooting the puck against Jim Watson. The Wales beat the Campbells 3–2, and I scored a goal for the winning side. Gilbert Perreault scored the winner in overtime in front of his hometown Sabres fans.

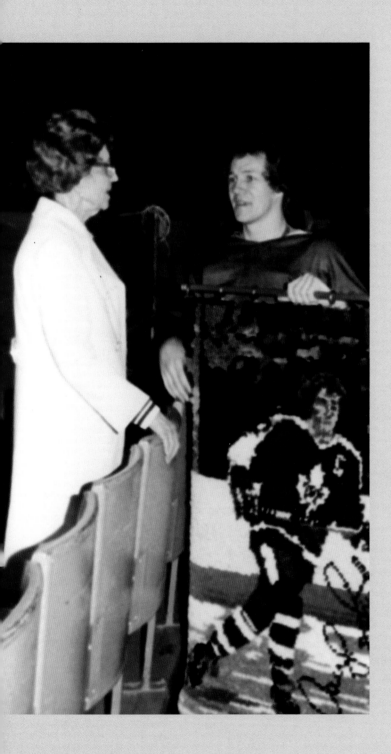

FANS

One morning at practice in 1979, a member of the Maple Leaf Gardens security staff came over to tell me that an older woman was waiting to see me. She was accompanied by her granddaughter, and they wanted to present me with a gift the woman had made at home. The woman's name was Florence Robertson, and the gift was a handmade rug featuring a picture of me in action. We took a photo together standing outside the Maple Leafs dressing room. I was so impressed by what she had done that I decided to try to get her a pair of tickets for the game that night – a playoff game at the Gardens against the Canadiens. I was able to pull it off, and she saw her first game at Maple Leaf Gardens! I still have the rug today.

Fans do all kinds of crazy things for their favourite teams and players. In Toronto, we got to know a particular group who were usually hanging around outside the Gardens. Sometimes they had gifts for us. I remember a large cookie made by a fan named Lena. She and a few others were a constant presence – and great fans. That cookie is long gone!

◀ Me, Florence Robertson, and the rug, 1979.

Holding a cookie from one of my biggest fans. ▶

THE CARTOON

Sometimes, a picture really is worth a thousand words. *Toronto Star* cartoonist Victor Roschkov very accurately summarized my life with the Maple Leafs after George "Punch" Imlach took over as general manager of the team in July 1979. In the image, Punch is on my back, wearing a button on his jacket that says, "I was Great in '58," while Harold Ballard has my stick all tied up, insisting, "Let's play hockey." In Harold's pocket is coach Floyd Smith, who can only say, "Yes."

"Who do you think you are?" Imlach asked the first time we met. He told me the team captain does what he tells them to do, and that he considered the player wearing the C to be part of management. He did not stop there. He told me he didn't like my agent, and that my "no-trade clause," which I had negotiated with Jim Gregory and Harold Ballard, was not valid. Punch banned me from participating in the *Hockey Night in Canada* intermission feature called "Showdown" (a skills competition), even though I had been involved for many seasons without any trouble. He kept me from being interviewed on *Hockey Night in Canada* (which I had also done on numerous occasions without incident) and did not like it when I did radio shows without his permission. Punch also wanted me to give up a vice-president position at the NHLPA.

Needless to say, I did not see eye to eye with Punch, and Harold backed him because he had just hired Imlach with the hope of recapturing the glory days of the 1960s, when Punch ran the Leafs. We had many more disagreements, and I told Punch exactly what I thought of his management style for the 1980s. He was furious and told me I was gone, that I would be traded. When he realized he couldn't do that, he traded away Lanny McDonald in late December of 1979. Lanny was not only the right winger on my line, he was also my best friend. Imlach had sent away many of the players who'd helped beat the New York Islanders in 1978, but when he traded Lanny (which in my view wasn't a hockey trade but a way to get back at me), that was pretty much it in terms of the Maple Leafs being a viable contender.

It was during the 1979–80 season that the organization insisted I take a week off and go to Florida. Coach Floyd Smith approached me with the idea and I told him I wasn't interested. Smitty, who was obviously in Imlach's corner and not someone I could trust, then said, "We can make you go." "You can't make me do anything," I replied. I just wanted to play hockey.

GIVING UP THE CAPTAINCY

On December 29, 1979, the Winnipeg Jets were in town for a Saturday night game against the Leafs. By this point I felt I had no communication with management and had decided it would be best to give up the captaincy. There were too many distractions surrounding the team and I believed stepping down would reduce some of the off-ice trouble. I recall telling Wendy what I was going to do. She advised me not to but my mind was made up.

I went out for the pre-game warm-up with the C still attached to my sweater. Back in the dressing room, though, I grabbed a scalpel and started to take it off by myself. But removing the C proved no easy task, thanks to the way it was stitched on my jersey. I had one of the trainers help me, telling him not to ask any questions, and we finally got it off. I had timed things perfectly, making sure we'd have just a few minutes before taking the ice, but on this night of all nights, the Zamboni broke down. We were stuck in the dressing room for more than half an hour.

We went out and beat the Jets 6–1 with Tiger Williams as the acting captain (he scored his 17th of the year, and Jerry Butler and I picked up an assist on the goal). After the game, I left copies of a note for the press that I had written earlier in the day, explaining why I took the action I did. I didn't want to speak directly to anyone; I just let the note do the talking for me.

On January 1, 1980, I had 28 points (11 goals, 17 assists) in 29 games played – I'd missed seven games with an injury – and was nowhere near the top 10 in the NHL scoring race. After I resigned the captaincy, I scored 29 goals and put up 40 assists to finish with 97 points on the season, ninth overall. Over the last 44 games of the season I recorded 69 points. Wayne Gretzky had 84 (to bring his season total to 137) over the last 45 games of his year, making us the two most productive players in the league over that time span. Marcel Dionne, who won the Art Ross Trophy (also with 137 points), had 65 points over the last 45 games of that 1979–80 season.

My two-page note to the media after giving up the captaincy (left); ▶
Pre-game warm-up on December 29, 1979 – still wearing the C (right).

27

DARRYL SITTLER

DEC 29/79

I TOLD MY TEAMATES AND MY COACH BEFORE THE GAME
THAT I WAS RESIGNING AS CAPTAIN OF THE TORONTO MAPLE
LEAFS.
WHEN I WAS MADE CAPTAIN, IT WAS THE HAPPIEST DAY OF
MY LIFE. I HAVE TRIED TO HANDLE MY DUTIES AS
CAPTAIN IN AN HONEST AND FAIR MANNER. I TOOK
PLAYER COMPLAINTS TO MANAGEMENT, AND DISCUSSED
MANAGEMENT IDEAS WITH PLAYERS.
AT THE START OF THIS SEASON, I WAS PERSONALLY SUED
BY MY OWN HOCKEY TEAM MANAGEMENT. I WAS TOLD
IT WAS NOTHING PERSONAL. I EXPLAINED MY POSITION
TO MR. IMLACH AND MR. BALLARD AT THAT TIME.
I TOLD THEM THAT I FELT A CAPTAIN'S ROLE WAS TO
WORK WITH PLAYERS AND MANAGEMENT, NOT JUST
MANAGEMENT.
MR. BALLARD AND MR. IMLACH MADE SOME NEGATIVE
COMMENTS ABOUT ME AND MY TEAMMATES SOME
WEEKS AGO AND I MET WITH THEM TO DISCUSS IT. I
WAS TOLD I WAS BEING TOO SENSITIVE.
I HAVE HAD LITTLE OR NO CONTACT WITH MR. IMLACH
AND IT IS CLEAR TO ME THAT HE AND I HAVE
DIFFERENT IDEAS ABOUT PLAYER AND MANAGEMENT
COMMUNICATION.
I HAVE RECENTLY BEEN TOLD THAT MANAGEMENT
HAS PREVENTED ME FROM APPEARING ON HOCKEY
NIGHT IN CANADA TELECASTS.

MANSOUR AND GILBERT — 200F PAD

CONN SMYTHE

When Conn Smythe died in November 1980, it was a sad day for the Maple Leafs – the organization and team Smythe had worked so hard to build, starting back in 1927. I was very aware of the Leafs' history and tradition under his leadership, so it was a great honour to be named one of the pallbearers at his funeral. Many former Leafs captains (such as Dave Keon, Syl Apps, Ted Kennedy, Jimmy Thomson, and Bob Davidson) were also asked to be pallbearers, and that made for a day I will always remember. The great legacy of the Maple Leafs may have been buried with Mr. Smythe, but his own reputation has remained untarnished since his passing.

I was at a dinner once where Mr. Smythe was also in attendance, and during my post-dinner talk, I used a bad word. Shortly afterward, I received a note from Mr. Smythe. In a very polite manner, he wrote that the captain of the Maple Leafs should never use bad language when speaking in public. He suggested next time I use the word *manure* instead. It might have been a bit old-fashioned but he was right, and I respected Mr. Smythe's wishes going forward.

During my early years with the team, my teammates and I would see Mr. Smythe around the Gardens. We didn't chat much – he always had a stern look on his face and was a little intimidating. In my first year as a Maple Leaf, team members were required to wear a shirt and tie to practice; that was the edict from Mr. Smythe. The rule was relaxed later on, but you had to appreciate that the man wanted to run his business in a certain way.

Two members of Mr. Smythe's family sent me a thank-you note after the funeral. Those notes are very meaningful to me, even to this day.

NOT INVITED TO CAMP

Perhaps I shouldn't have been surprised when I didn't get invited to training camp in the fall of 1980, but it did have me wondering, especially since my no-trade agreement was still in place. Punch was certainly behind the move. When he suffered a heart attack in August, however, I asked to meet directly with Harold Ballard. Ballard told me that Punch was out as general manager – he would find something else for Imlach to do, even if it meant driving the Zamboni. Harold explained that he had to back Imlach, since he had given him the general manager's job, and that he was sorry for how things had gone during the previous season. Assured that Punch was gone, I took back the captaincy when it was offered and we held a press conference to announce my return to the team.

I had a pretty good year in 1980–81, with 96 points, but the team was still in disarray and we managed only 28 wins. The New York Islanders wiped us out in three games in the opening round of the playoffs. At this point I had little confidence in the future of the team, but they had signed Borje Salming, Wilf Paiement, Pat Hickey, and Ian Turnbull to new contracts. I thought I deserved a new deal as well. At the start of the season, I had talked to Harold about the possibility of renegotiating my contract. He promised to re-evaluate my contractual status, although he noted that there'd be a board of directors meeting before he could say anything for sure.

And so, on the day of the board meeting, I waited in a local restaurant for my follow-up meeting with Ballard. I called to confirm a meeting that afternoon, and, the only thing he could do for me, Ballard said, was trade me elsewhere. That phone call ended my time with the Leafs, though I had to wait until the January 20, 1982, before a deal was finally completed.

132   **With Ballard at the press conference announcing my return to the team.** ▶

1396 Birchwood Drive
Mississauga, Ontario
L5J 1T2

December 30, 1981

Mr. Harold E. Ballard
President and Managing Director
Toronto Maple Leafs
Maple Leaf Gardens
60 Carlton Street
Toronto, Ontario
M5B 1L1

Dear Mr. Ballard:

In September, I asked you to review my contract in view of the
contract deals Mr. Imlach had made with some of my teammates. You
agreed at that time that I deserved consideration and that you would
consider my position. You told me that you knew many general managers
who had renegotiated contracts of their top players. You told me you
appreciated my off-ice commitments to Maple Leaf Gardens and to the
City of Toronto, and my involvement with charities. You told me you
would talk to the Board of Directors and get back to me.

In October, I met you again and you asked me what I wanted. I told
you I would like the type of salary you gave Borje Salming or an
extension of my contract. I told you we could sit down and talk
the figures and terms over and that I would be fair with you and the
Leafs.

Later in October, I went to meet with you in your office. While I
was waiting in the lobby of the executive offices you told me in front
of the office staff that you had spoken to some Board members and
that it didn't look as if anything could be done for me.

Later that day in your office, you told me that you would give it
another try at a Board meeting on November 9th. I asked you if I
could come to the Board meeting and explain my feelings to the
Directors. You told me this was not possible.

At that same meeting, you told me that you had a lot of players you
wanted to trade, but couldn't trade because you would get nothing
for them. I told you that you could get something for me. You told
me you didn't want to trade me and I told you I wanted to finish my

Continued...

▲
My December 1981 letter to Ballard.   133

MEETING TERRY FOX

I first heard of Terry Fox in the spring of 1980, when he started his "Marathon of Hope" by dipping his artificial leg in the Atlantic Ocean. I read in the newspaper that he was going to run 26 miles every day (and I thought my five-mile runs were pretty good!). I followed Terry's progress like so many Canadians were doing, until I got a phone call one day from the Canadian Cancer Society. They wanted to do something special for Terry as he hit the Ontario/Quebec border, and they recalled that Terry had once said he wanted to meet me and Bobby Orr. I was more than happy to help, and when I agreed, they asked me to keep it quiet so Terry would be surprised.

July 11, 1980, was a beautiful summer day. On the way down to Toronto from my cottage in Orillia, I thought about what I could give Terry as a gift. Finally, I came up with what I hoped was a great idea. After a quick stop at home to pick up my 1980 NHL All-Star Game sweater, I went off to the designated spot. I met Terry at the 13-mile mark that day in the Yorkville district of Toronto, and a big smile came over his face when he saw me. I asked him if he wanted to go for a run. The organizers gave me a "Marathon of Hope" T-shirt and off we ran until we got to Nathan Phillips Square at Toronto's City Hall. It was there that I gave Terry the sweater with the number 27 on the back. By the time he put it on, we both had tears in our eyes. The crowd that greeted Terry was tremendous (an estimated 10,000 people), and it has been written that he raised $100,000 in donations on that day alone.

When we were out in Vancouver early in the 1980–81 season, we invited Terry into the Maple Leaf dressing room and he met all the guys on the team. We all tried to encourage him, but you could see that the return of the cancer had affected him physically. He died in June 1981.

Later on, when renowned Canadian artist Ken Danby was commissioned to do a painting of Terry's journey, he included Terry wearing my sweater as part of the montage. The Danby drawing hangs in Ottawa. There were no copies made, but Ken took a picture of the painting for me and I had it framed. It hangs proudly in my home and I think of Terry every time I walk past. I might have been one of his favourite hockey players, but he quickly became an inspirational hero to me. Terry decided he was going to make a difference and he did – not only in Canada but around the world. Since he started his marathon back in 1980, he has raised over $600 million worldwide for cancer research – and donations to the Terry Fox Foundation still pour in each year. To me, Terry Fox is the greatest Canadian ever.

◀ **At Nathan Phillips Square in Toronto.**

PASSING KEON AND SETTING NEW TEAM MARKS

In March 1981, I set three new team marks for the Maple Leafs. The first came against the Calgary Flames on March 7, 1981, when my 494th career assist topped Dave Keon's mark of 493. One night later, on March 8, I had two assists during a game against Mike Palmateer and the Washington Capitals to pass Keon's club record of 858 points. On March 14, 1981, during a home game against the very same Capitals, I scored career goals 365, 366, and 367 to pass another team record (365) held by Keon. The goal that set the new mark was assisted by Bruce Boudreau. My hat trick that night came against Palmateer. We won the contest 5–3 but Mike was out of the net for the last goal since the Capitals had pulled the goalie late to try to tie the game.

"THAT'S NICE BUT I'D SOONER WIN A STANLEY CUP."

Darryl Sittler on being told he had passed Dave Keon's team record for most career goals, March 14, 1981

Dave Keon was a player I greatly admired for all he had done in his illustrious NHL career, and he was a teammate for the first five years I was in the league. Breaking his club records for most goals, assists, and points was very special for me.

Versus Palmateer in the Washington net on March 14, 1981, ▶
the night I set the Maple Leafs team record for most career goals.

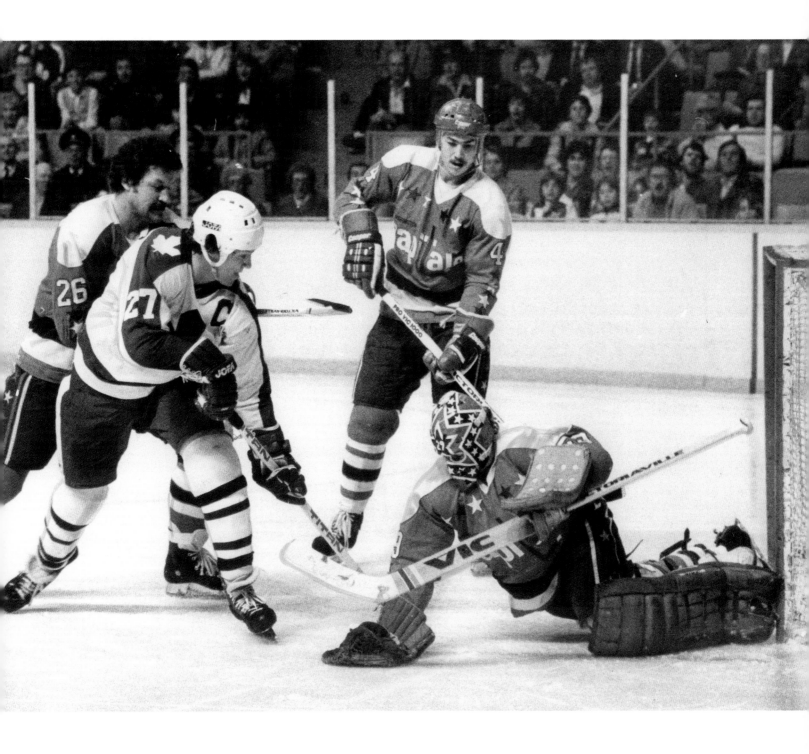

The Hockey News

$1.25   64522   THE INTERNATIONAL HOCKEY WEEKLY   MARCH 11, 1983   Vol. 36, No. 22

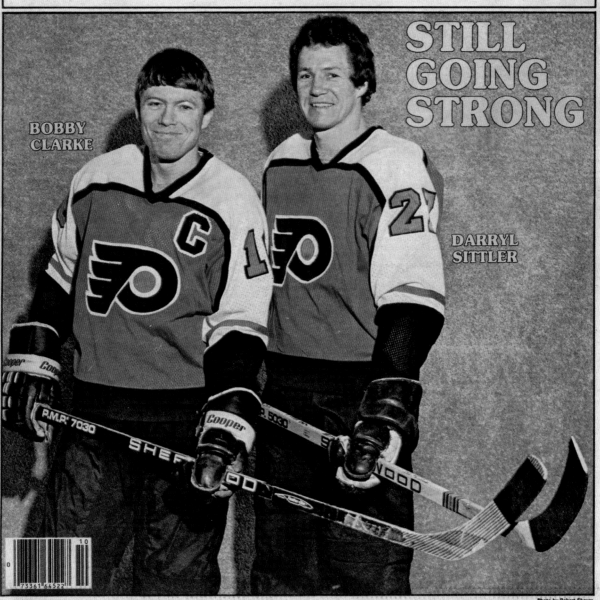

STILL GOING STRONG

BOBBY CLARKE

DARRYL SITTLER

THE TRADE TO PHILADELPHIA

So Harold Ballard didn't even think I was worthy of a face-to-face meeting to tell me I wasn't getting a new contract. I immediately went down to see general manager Gerry McNamara and told him I would accept a deal to Minnesota or Philadelphia. McNamara tried to calm me down and said he would speak to Ballard but my mind was made up. We agreed to keep the situation quiet, but when Alan Eagleson was interviewed after a Maple Leafs/Canadiens Saturday night game on December 12, 1981, he told everyone watching *Hockey Night in Canada* that the game was likely my final one in a Toronto uniform. Although this got a lot of media attention, I preferred not to comment.

The situation dragged on for more than a month, and I decided after consulting with two doctors that I needed some stress relief. Even though I had two medical notes, McNamara threated to suspend me. I played my final game as a Maple Leaf on January 2, 1982, staying away from the team until a deal was done with Philadelphia on January 20.

I made the Flyers one of my choices because they were always competitive and I thought they had a chance to win a Stanley Cup – coach Pat Quinn had taken the Flyers to the Stanley Cup final in 1980. I was also impressed with owner Ed Snider, who I knew from my work with the Players' Association. The expectations would be high, but I didn't mind that at all.

Even though the Leafs and the Flyers had been bitter rivals, I had no trouble fitting in in the Philadelphia dressing room. The transition was made much easier thanks to the mutual respect we had for each other as competitors. It was a good change for me. Everything was handled in a first-class way, and the spotlight was not nearly as bright as it was in Toronto. That made for much less scrutiny, which was nice.

1982 WORLD HOCKEY CHAMPIONSHIPS

When the Maple Leafs traded me to Philadelphia on January 20, 1982, I played in 35 games for the Flyers to close out the 1981–82 season and recorded 32 points (14 goals, 18 assists). The Flyers finished the year with 38 wins and 87 points and were favoured to beat the Rangers in the opening round of the playoffs but they beat us three games to one and I was soon off to join Team Canada for the 1982 World Hockey Championships, played in Helsinki, Finland. We had a pretty good team that featured players like Bobby Clarke, Bill Barber, Rick Vaive, Mike Gartner, and Dale Hawerchuk. I had a good tournament and scored four goals and totalled seven points in 10 games played. It felt good to represent my country once again.

Bill Barber was a bit of an underrated player throughout his NHL career, being in the shadow of Bobby Clarke and later Reggie Leach. However, he was an important player on the Flyers' top line. He had a great snap shot and was a good playmaker on the attack. Many people did not like him because he was seen as a diver but that was part of his competitive nature. I got to know Barber a little because we had the same agent, and when I got traded to Philadelphia, Wendy and I stayed with Bill and Jenny Barber for the first while. Barber scored eight goals (in 10 games) during the Helsinki tournament, which saw Team Canada win a bronze medal. His solid NHL play (including 420 career goals) was recognized when he was elected to the Hall of Fame in 1990.

Wayne Gretzky was also my teammate at the 1982 World Championships and he had two goals and two assists in the final game, which we won 6–0 over Sweden to come home with a bronze medal. Gretzky had a total of 14 points in the tournament. After one of the contests I was named the player of the game and they gave me a wrist watch. Since I had accumulated so many watches over the years I passed this one along onto to Gretzky. The only problem was a Canadian customs agent was watching the game and asked me about the watch when we were trying to clear customs. I managed to smooth everything over and still not tell the agent that Gretzky had the goods!

In a Team Canada uniform at WHC in 1982 (left); ▶
With Clarke and Barber on Team Canada (right).

"IT'S A NICE GOAL TO REACH. IF I HAD DONE IT IN TORONTO, I WOULD HAVE BEEN THE FIRST LEAF TO REACH SUCH A GOAL. BUT I DID IT HERE [IN PHILADELPHIA] AND I GOT A NICE RECEPTION THAT I APPRECIATED VERY MUCH . . . I'VE PLAYED 13 YEARS WITHOUT MY NAME ON THE STANLEY CUP BUT I THINK I HAVE A GOOD CHANCE WITH THIS CLUB." **Sittler on the night he recorded his 1,000th career point**

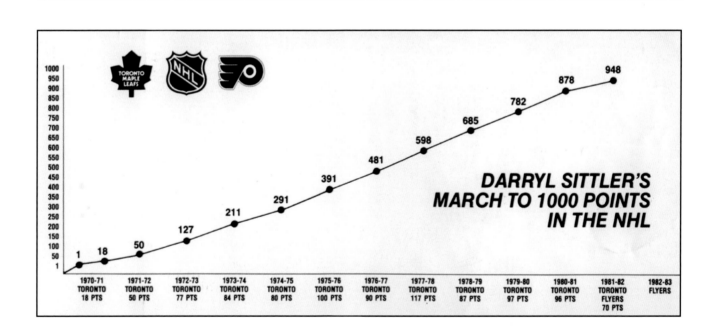

DARRYL SITTLER'S MARCH TO 1000 POINTS IN THE NHL

MY 1,000TH CAREER POINT

On January 20, 1983, exactly one year to the day that I was traded from Toronto to Philadelphia, I recorded my 1,000th career point, becoming just the 17th player in NHL history to achieve the milestone. The game was played in Philadelphia against Calgary, and my great buddy Lanny McDonald was in uniform for the Flames that night. I got my 999th point in the first period, when I assisted on a goal by Glen Cochrane. Then, in the third, I was assisted by Bill Barber and Brad Marsh when I let a shot go that beat Don Edwards in the Calgary net.

My 1,000 points were made up of 433 goals and 567 assists. The goal I scored was the 30th of the year for me and marked the 10th straight season I had scored 30 or more. The Flyers were very classy about recognizing the moment. They released the sheet you see on the right from the ceiling so fans could have a souvenir of the achievement.

Turns out another amazing thing happened that night. A young lady in her early 20s was in the hospital and in a coma due to a brain aneurysm. Since she and her family were big Flyers fans, they had placed a television in her room at the foot of the bed for watching games. She told me that at the exact moment I recorded my 1,000th point, she awoke and came out of her coma!

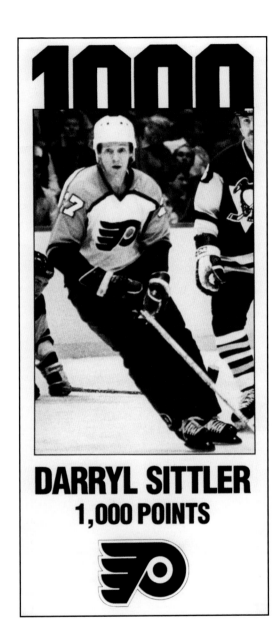

DARRYL SITTLER
1,000 POINTS

RETURN TO TORONTO AS A FLYER

The Maple Leafs traded me to Philadelphia on January 20, 1982, but because of the schedule, I didn't return to Toronto until March 2, 1983. I was greeted warmly by fans away from the rink and gave plenty of media interviews before the game. I didn't get on the ice until almost seven minutes into the game. I would have preferred to get on quickly, just to get the nerves out, but Flyers coach Bob McCammon thought it would be better to wait and give me a chance to relax.

The reaction when I skated out was mixed – some cheers, some boos. It had been quite a while since I'd left, and the parting had featured a lot of controversy, so maybe that's why the fans seemed indifferent. At the time, there was no tradition of welcome-back videos, like there is today for some players. I wasn't disappointed by the reaction and just took it in stride. Philadelphia was never a popular team in Toronto anyway. The game finished 2–2 and Mike Palmateer of the Leafs made two good saves to keep me off the scoreboard.

In this photo I am wearing the Cooperalls style of pants, though I didn't like them. I preferred the traditional short, loose pants that allowed me to put on my skates and shin guards first. The Cooperalls came with protective gear inside the pants, and if you fell on the ice with them on you slid too much. Flyers owner Ed Snider was an innovator, the type of guy who liked to try new things, and the Flyers and the Hartford Whalers were the two NHL teams testing the Cooperalls out. I was glad when this experiment faded away rather quickly. It was a non-traditional hockey look and it never caught on in the rest of the league.

Wearing the Cooperalls. ▶

"I KNEW PALMY WAS GOING TO
COME OUT SO I TRIED TO PUT
THE PUCK UP HIGH . . ."

**Darryl Sittler on being stymied by Maple Leafs netminder
Mike Palmateer during his first game against Toronto as a Flyer**

"I HAD A LOT OF GOOD MEMORIES HERE.
IT WAS NICE TO SEE THE GARDENS AND
THE PEOPLE WHO WORK HERE.
IT'S NICE TO SEE FRIENDS."

Darryl Sittler on his return to Toronto in March of 1983

1983 IN WEST GERMANY

After a pretty good year in 1982–83, the Philadelphia Flyers were once again knocked out of the Stanley Cup playoffs by the New York Rangers. (I scored 43 goals and had 83 points in my first full year with the team.) The Flyers had won 49 games and recorded 106 points, while the Rangers had won only 35 games and recorded 80 points. However, New York coach Herb Brooks had his players ready for the post-season and they beat us in three straight games in the best-of-five division semifinal. Once again it was off to Europe to play for Canada, this time at the 1983 World Hockey Championships in West Germany.

Dave King was coaching Team Canada for the second consecutive season, and Marcel Dionne, Bob Gainey, Michel Goulet, Scott Stevens, and Brian Propp were on the squad. I scored three times in 10 games, and we once again came home with a bronze medal. The four teams to make it to the medal round were Canada, Sweden, Czechoslovakia, and the Soviet Union. The only game we won in the medal round came against Sweden, when we beat them 3–1. We lost to the Czechs 5–4 and to the Soviet Union 8–2. I never really liked playing on the larger ice surfaces in Europe. I found you couldn't get as involved in the play as on the smaller North American rinks, which I had grown used to over my playing career. We did medal in both years I played in the world tournament, and considering Team Canada is put together at pretty much the last minute – where many of the other teams gear up much further ahead and take the competition very seriously – I think we did rather well. Given the rigours of the NHL season, it's always difficult for Team Canada to win it all.

With team captain Marcel Dionne at 1983 World Championships. ▶

ANOTHER TRADE

In the summer before the 1983–84 season, the Flyers discussed the team captaincy with me. I was pleased to accept the role. Bobby Clarke had retired and taken over the management of the Flyers (he wanted to be called "Bob" from that point on). We talked about announcing my new role over the summer, but it was delayed until training camp because the Sutter twins, Rich and Ron, were unable to attend and the team wanted to do one press conference to reveal their signing and my captaincy. In the meantime, I met with new coach Mike Keenan. Everything went well.

The announcement was finally going to be made at an organization luncheon. Five hundred people were expected to attend, including many of the Flyers' corporate sponsors. I had my speech ready and actually did interviews prior to the event where I acknowledged that I was getting the C put on my orange-and-black jersey. However, the luncheon came and went. I was not asked to speak and there was no announcement made. I was definitely surprised, and wondered what was going on.

Coach Mike Keenan asked me to go to his office, and I had no idea why. When I got there, Bobby Clarke was waiting for me, and I was told that a deal had been completed with the Red Wings. I was shocked and told him I wasn't going. I could have pursued free agency over the off-season, I reminded him, but chose to stay when the Flyers said they wanted me back. Clarke said he had to make what he thought was a good deal for the team (and he was right in that respect, because Murray Craven, who came to the Flyers in the trade, was a very good player), but that didn't make me feel any better. To top it all off, Clarke even refused to say that I had been given the captaincy. He would only concede that I was one of the players being considered!

Maybe Clarke's inexperience as a general manager was evident in how he handled the whole situation. Whatever the case may be, I told him exactly what I thought of it all.

A YEAR WITH THE RED WINGS

Detroit had been pursuing me for some time, going back to my battles in Toronto with Punch Imlach. Back then, they'd offered me $500,000 to waive my no-trade clause and come play for them. As tempting as that was, I turned it down. I wanted to show everyone that I could outlast Imlach in Toronto. Once I made the decision to report to Detroit after the trade from Philadelphia, I found that playing for the Red Wings wasn't a great experience.

Detroit actually had an interesting team in 1984–85. Veterans such as Brad Park, Danny Gare, Ron Duguay, Ivan Boldirev, and my old buddy Tiger Williams were there. They also had some good young players coming onto the team in Steve Yzerman, Gerard Gallant, Kelly Kisio, and goalie Greg Stefan. However, coach Nick Polano did not see me as a contributor over the length of the season, and even though he asked for my input, he didn't really want to hear what I had to say. This despite the fact I had put up 63 points in my last season as a Flyer.

Early in the season during a game in Toronto, a serious injury set me back. Jim Korn was a big physical presence on the Maple Leafs. We may have had a few run-ins prior to October 24, 1984. This time, though, Korn hit me from behind and drove my head into the dasher along the top of the boards. It was a bad injury to the cheekbone and eye area, with the eye slipping down too far into the socket. I managed to take a swipe at Korn before I was rushed off to the hospital to get the broken orbital bone damage repaired.

While I was lying on a stretcher in emergency, my father was wheeled in through the front doors. He had suffered a heart attack while attending the game. My father ended up in intensive care and I was scheduled for surgery the next morning. I recovered and managed to play in 61 games that year, scoring 11 goals and totalling 27 points. One of my best performances came in Toronto on March 6, 1985, when the Red Wings beat the Leafs 5–3. I scored two goals and had one assist despite wearing a face mask to protect my injury. The first goal came with Korn in the penalty box. Steve Yzerman assisted on my second goal, which was the game winner (the second time I had done that to the Maple Leafs that season). I was selected the first star of the game, marking the only time I'd received that honour while not wearing a Toronto uniform. Detroit made the playoffs; the Maple Leafs did not.

Wearing the protective face mask at Maple Leaf Gardens. ▶

"IT'S VERY GRATIFYING FOR ME TO BE
ABLE TO CONTRIBUTE TO THIS TEAM
AND SCORE IN THIS BUILDING . . .
I WANTED TO PROVE THAT I CAN STILL
PLAY, ESPECIALLY IN TORONTO."

Darryl Sittler after Detroit's
win over Toronto, March 6, 1985

FINAL GAME AND RETIREMENT

Detroit played Chicago in the opening round of the 1985 playoffs and the Black Hawks took us out in three straight. I played in the first two games of the series, but when the second game ended I had a feeling I was not going to play the next. I was right: I was not dressed for the third game, which ended up making April 11, 1985, my final game in the NHL.

However, I didn't know it at the time. I had every intention of completing my two-year contract with the Red Wings. I went to meet with general manager Jim Devellano. I wanted to tell him that I wasn't the player they had seen in 1984–85. I wanted to tell him that so many things had gone wrong that year (including the unexpected trade from Philadelphia, my eye injury, and the death of my father) and they had all affected my performance. Before I could say anything, though, I was told the Red Wings were letting many of the veterans go and that the team was buying me out. There was no discussion – the decision was final.

Vancouver wanted to sign me for the 1985–86 season, but one beautiful August morning I went out for a run and decided I would take the payout and call it a career. It was not an easy decision, especially with an offer from the Canucks on the table and just 16 goals short of 500 career markers. Only 10 players in NHL history had scored that many goals prior to the start of the 1985–86 campaign. It would have been nice to end my career on a better note, but in the end I thought my choice to leave the game was best for me and my family.

As a Red Wing in my final NHL season. ▶

London Nationals reunion.

SEVEN

HONOURS

RETIRING #9

On March 28, 1988, the London Knights honoured me by retiring my sweater number 9 before a playoff game against the Sault Ste. Marie Greyhounds. With Wendy and my children looking on, I was presented with a framed sweater as a keepsake of the event. It was a very emotional night for me, since it brought me back to the days of my youth – I even met people who had been working at the arena since my playing days! The Knights were celebrating 25 years at the London Gardens and I was the first player to have a sweater number retired. In my first season, the team was called the Nationals and the logo was the multi-point Maple Leaf (the team had started out as a Toronto junior affiliate, replacing St. Michael's College in the Leafs' junior system). When Howard Darwin bought the team the name was changed to Knights.

That evening, the Knights also took time to select the all-time MVP and a first and second all-star team through a contest with the fans. I was honoured to be named the MVP and secure a spot on the first all-star team along with Dan Maloney, Dino Ciccarelli, Rob Ramage, Brad Marsh, and goalie Pat Riggin. Since then, the Knights have retired the sweater numbers of Ramage, Marsh, Ciccarelli, Brendan Shanahan, Rick Nash, Corey Perry, and Dave Bolland. The Knights won the Memorial Cup in 2005 for the very first time.

In 2015, there was a reunion of Nationals and Knights players to celebrate 50 years of major junior hockey in London, Ontario. It was great to see such a gathering; it brought back many wonderful memories.

"THIS SURE BRINGS BACK A LOT OF WARM MEMORIES . . . I ALWAYS TRIED TO LEAD A LIFE THAT WOULD BE A POSITIVE INFLUENCE ON PEOPLE. I WAS BY NO MEANS PERFECT, BUT IF THAT NUMBER 9 HANGING THERE CAN HELP SOMEONE, THEN I FEEL GOOD ABOUT IT." **Darryl Sittler on March 28, 1988**

INDUCTION TO
THE HOCKEY HALL OF FAME

It was Jim Gregory who called to tell me I was going to be a Hall of Fame inductee in 1989. Hearing the news from Jim was especially nice, since he had been such a big part of my hockey career. A few days after this good news came in, we got a different type of call altogether: Wendy's mother, Eve Bibbings, had suffered a terrible stroke while on vacation in England. She used my induction date as motivation to get better, and she was indeed at the ceremony, sitting in a wheelchair.

It was a great night. My family was there, along with some other special people. One of those was my childhood hero, Jean Béliveau, and I got his autograph that night. He came up on stage at the end of the evening with all of the other Hall of Fame players in attendance. What a special moment, to know that I was now a member of this group. My best friend, Lanny McDonald, was also there with his wife, Ardell. Lanny was my presenter and he closed his speech in this manner: "Tonight we honour Darryl Sittler as a great hockey player who made history happen. I honour Darryl Sittler as a man I'm proud to call my best friend."

With the McDonalds on induction night (top); ▶
With fellow HHOF member Jean Béliveau at the NHL Alumni Golf Tournament (bottom).

MICHAEL BURGESS

I got to know singer Michael Burgess when he began singing the national anthem at Maple Leaf Gardens. Usually, he would get the most important contests, like opening night or playoff games. Coach Pat Burns was especially superstitious about having Michael sing the anthem before certain games; he considered him a good luck charm. Sometimes Burgess would sing at the Gardens and then rush to the theatre for the opening curtain of *Les Misérables*, to take the stage as Jean Valjean.

In addition to being a renowned world-class singer, Burgess was big sports fan and something of a hockey player. He often joined the hockey legends as we travelled across Canada and would play in the charity game. He would also sing at the intermissions. Instead of sitting in the dressing room, we would come out to hear Michael perform some of his most famous renditions, such as "Danny Boy."

Michael gave Wendy some of his CDs and DVDs, and one song in particular, "I Love You Forever," became a favourite around our house. When Wendy came home on Thanksgiving weekend in 2001, we all knew she was near the end of her life. We had no definite idea of how long she would be with us, but we were so grateful to have her home one last time.

With Ryan, Meaghan, Ashley, and I gathered around her in her room, I decided to step out for a minute to put on "I Love You Forever," since I knew she loved it so much. When I came back to her room, Wendy took a couple of breaths and then passed away as the song continued. That is how she died at home. It was a very emotional time for all of us. We hadn't known how the end would come, but with the Michael Burgess song playing, it was a beautiful, peaceful ending to her life.

With Michael Burgess at the Air Canada Centre. ▶

My family and I look on as
the banner is raised to the roof.

SITTLER
27

RAISING THE BANNER

On September 15, 2001, Ken Dryden, who had taken over from Cliff Fletcher as the Leafs' general manager, called me at home. He said the team wanted to recognize Frank Mahovlich and me by honouring our sweater number (we both wore 27). The team was celebrating its 75th anniversary that season, and this would be part of the festivities. The Leafs had started honouring players in the early 1990s, and I was very proud to join the impressive and growing group. However, I had to tell Ken that my wife, Wendy, was very ill and I didn't think it was going to be possible for me to participate. Frank's banner was raised on October 3, 2001, the opening night of the new season. Wendy died just three days later, on October 6, over the Canadian Thanksgiving holiday weekend.

Wendy had the most impact on my life, and she supported me every day and was very serious about helping me. She was a great mom to Ryan, Meaghan, and Ashley and a great wife to me and I respected her in every way. She was also very conscious about her role as the wife of the team captain; she always tried hard to make everyone feel welcome. With all of this in mind, I decided I wanted Wendy's name to be included on my banner. This request naturally caught Dryden off guard. He said he would consider it, but would have to get the idea approved. They didn't want to start a precedent that they couldn't manage in the future.

At first, the organization came back with an idea I really did not like. Wendy's name could go on the banner but it would be a secret between me, my family, and a few in management. They would add Wendy's name – in blue – to the blue sweater I was pictured wearing on the banner. I said no to that suggestion, while still being adamant about including Wendy's name. I told them it didn't have to be large but that I wanted it to be seen. It wouldn't hurt anyone, and it was important to me. I found a written note with her signature on it and they decided to go ahead with the plan. Wendy's name would appear in blue along the white stripe at the bottom of my Maple Leafs sweater.

I picked February 8, 2003, for the banner raising – a Saturday night game against Montreal that would be broadcast on *Hockey Night in Canada*. It was also just one day after the 27th anniversary of my 10-point game. Ryan, Meaghan, and Ashley were with me that night, and I mentioned in my speech that Wendy was with us in spirit. The reaction from the crowd at the ACC was great, and there weren't too many dry eyes in the house. I love the fact that when people look up at the ACC rafters, they can see Wendy's name on the banner. I accomplished many things over my years in hockey, but I consider this night to be the greatest moment of my career.

◀ My banner at the ACC.

LEGENDS ROW

When you consider that the Maple Leafs will be celebrating 100 years as a National Hockey League franchise in 2017, it's only fitting that they establish a site like Legends Row outside of their home arena. People from all across Canada used to visit Maple Leaf Gardens when the team played there; now they come to the Air Canada Centre. Legends Row will allow those visitors to celebrate the long history of the team and the great players honoured along the special "bench" that has been created. It's also a great spot to snap a picture or two to share with others. The bronze statue erected in my honour is a curly-haired (good work by artist Erik Blome) rendition of me in my playing days, jumping over the boards. It's sort of an action shot – which I think is pretty cool!

Last summer, my grandson Luke was in for a visit and we decided to go down to a Blue Jays game. After the game, it was a nice summer night, and I said to my wife, Luba, "Let's go snap some photos at Legends Row. I want to get a shot of Luke with my statue." When we got over there, we found some teenagers climbing on the back of my statue! "Hey, get off there," I said to one kid. (I thought he was going to break it.) "Show a little respect for this area. This is not a toy." He had no idea that was a statue of me. Just then, a bus full of tourists showed up and they all came right up and asked for autographs and pictures. I think it may have finally dawned on this kid that I was the statue!

"THE FANS OF LEAFS NATION LOVE PLAYERS OF CHARACTER WHO ARE HARD-WORKING AND KIND OF HUMBLE. THAT'S ALL THEY EXPECT, AND THEN, IF YOU PUT A WINNING TEAM ON THE ICE, THEY WILL SUPPORT YOU UNBELIEVABLY . . . [LEGENDS ROW] IS SOMETHING THAT WILL BE THERE A LONG TIME."

Darryl Sittler, at the unveiling of his statue on September 6, 2014

Beside my statue at the Air Canada Centre (top); With my family at Legends Row (bottom). ▶

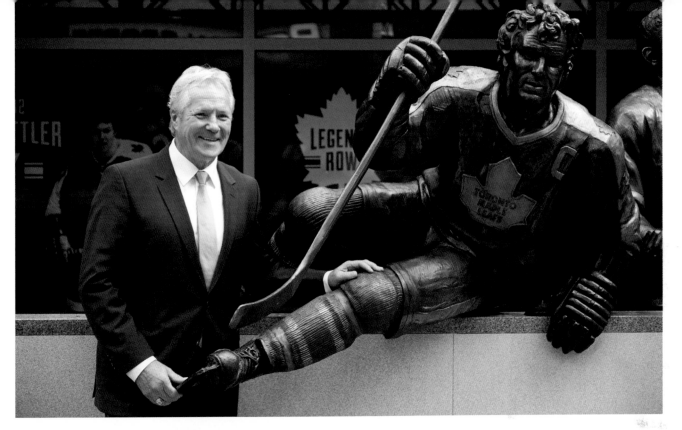

MAPLE LEAFS ALUMNI

It was not all that long ago that the Maple Leafs alumni didn't really exist. Sure, ex-players were around, but they weren't generally welcomed back during the Harold Ballard years (except for a few former Leafs who were employed by the team). Cliff Fletcher changed all that (with the approval of new owner Steve Stavro) when he took over as team president, and the alumni have been an important part of the organization since the early 1990s. There are now over 200 members and the group is very involved in Toronto and its surrounding communities.

One of the biggest events in the history of the alumni was the Winter Classic, put on by the NHL over the New Year period to start 2014. The Leafs alumni were included in the outdoor event, held at Comerica Park in Detroit, and a few of us even brought our grandsons along. There was so much interest that two alumni games were played, and two alumni team photos were taken that day. We made sure that the alumni who typically play in many local and community games were able to get to Detroit and participate in this major event, which got a lot of media coverage. I will always remember Gordie Howe and Ted Lindsay dropping the puck between Steve Yzerman and me to get the alumni game going. We had at least three generations of hockey players participating in the two games, and it was a wonderful experience.

◀ Ceremonial puck drop with Steve Yzerman, Gordie Howe, and Ted Lindsay at Comerica Park, 2014 (left);
With grandson Luke on our way to the Winter Classic (right).

MAPLE LEAFS CAPTAINS AND TEAM RECORDS

Back in June of 2005, nine Maple Leaf captains gathered together for a limited-edition photo. Ted Kennedy, George Armstrong, Dave Keon, Rick Vaive, Rob Ramage, Wendel Clark, Doug Gilmour, and Mats Sundin were there with me and we eventually signed each copy of the 1,000 lithographs made. The lithograph was entitled "Captain's Row" and sales helped raise money for charities. There is always great respect among the captains of the Maple Leafs because each of us understands the tradition that goes with the honour of being the captain of the Toronto Maple Leafs. It is not often that you can gather everyone like this together but it was nice to share stories with all of the Toronto captains and get a better appreciation of each player.

Team records and NHL records are in my view a function of the era you play in and who you play with in your career. I was fortunate enough to set some team records while I was with the Maple Leafs, such as most points in one season when I had 117 in 1977–78. It stayed as the team record until the 1992–93 season, when Doug Gilmour had a great year and finished with 127. As much as you might like for the record to stay yours, it is inevitable that someone will come along at some point and break your mark. Doug Gilmour was my favourite player when he was with the Maple Leafs and being in team management at the time allowed me to see this small, competitive, tenacious fan favourite set the new team record up close.

I was also involved in the discussions when Cliff Fletcher was thinking about trading for Mats Sundin. I was all in favour of bringing in the big Swede to the Maple Leafs, although I hated to see another one of my favourites in Wendel Clark go the other way in the deal with Quebec. Sundin broke many of my team marks including most goals, most points, and most seasons leading the team in scoring. When great players set new marks you have to admire what they have done, just like others may have had high regard for what I had achieved years ago. Both Doug and Mats have been elected to the Hockey Hall of Fame, which indicates what great players they were in their time in the NHL.

Leaf captains gather for a limited-edition photo (top); ▶
With former Leaf captains Armstrong, Phaneuf, and Clark (bottom).

CAPTAINS ROW KENNEDY · CAPTAINS ROW ARMSTRONG · CAPTAINS ROW KEON · CAPTAINS ROW SITTLER · CAPTAINS ROW VAIVE · CAPTAINS ROW RAMAGE · CAPTAINS ROW CLARK · CAPTAINS ROW GILMOUR · CAPTAINS ROW SUNDIN

Brendan Shanahan's Hockey Idols card. ▶

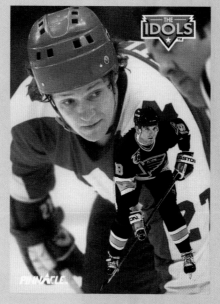

248 THE IDOLS ™ ★★★

BRENDAN SHANAHAN **DARRYL SITTLER**

Like a lot of boys in the Toronto area, Brendan looked up to former Maple Leaf captain Darryl Sittler. One of the league's hardest workers, Darryl spent 12 seasons with the Leafs from 1970-82 and still ranks as the club's all-time leader in goals (389) and points (916). He led Toronto in scoring eight consecutive years and was elected to the Hockey Hall of Fame in 1989.

PINNACLE ™

Shanahan filling me in on the Legends Row
▼ project and the plans for my statue.

BRENDAN SHANAHAN

In 1976 I bought a home in Mississauga, Ontario, and lived there until I was traded from the Maple Leafs to the Flyers. There was a pond in the backyard and in the winter it would become a skating rink for my kids. Other kids heard about it and would often come over to skate and play hockey – especially when I was not at home. One of those kids was a young man named Brendan Shanahan. Turns out I was his hockey hero. He was raised in Mimico, Ontario, but he'd heard about the Sittler rink through his friends and they all came out to Mississauga. A few years ago, the card pictured here came out. It was the first time that I became aware that Brendan had listed me as his hockey idol. I always liked the way Shanahan played the game, which I thought was very similar to my style.

When Brendan took over as president of the Maple Leafs in April 2014, one of his first duties was to put together a Legends Row of statues outside Air Canada Centre, recognizing some of the great players who had suited up in Toronto. I was honoured to be one of the first selected.

"I LIKED THE WAY [SITTLER] PLAYED AND THE WAY HE CARRIED HIMSELF AS A PROFESSIONAL."
Brendan Shanahan, September 2015

Brendan and I share a few other connections: We both played junior hockey in London, and both of our sweaters are honoured by the Knights. We also have some mutual friends, including player agent Rick Curran. When I first started attending the Orr-Walton Sports Camp in the summers, it was Curran who would come by and pick me up in a limousine for the ride to Orillia, Ontario. I sat up in the front with Rick and got to know the man who would eventually become Brendan Shanahan's agent. Curran and Bill Watters (one of my hockey agents) were the first two to tell me about a young player in London who was going to be an NHL star. It's funny how life can circle around like that, revealing surprising connections between yourself and the people you know.

CLOSING OF MAPLE LEAF GARDENS

The closing of Maple Leaf Gardens on February 13, 1999, was a nice celebration – whether you were inside the building, where the official ceremony was taking place, or outside, where many of us did live interviews.

For me, it was a time of mixed emotions; after all, I had practically lived at the place for many years. But the organizers did a good job of making sure that players past and present had a chance to say a proper goodbye. All of the Hall of Fame players in attendance were introduced, and we stood at the points on the Maple Leaf logo, which was a nice touch. A highlight of the closing ceremonies was Canadian superstar Anne Murray singing "The Maple Leaf Forever" to end the evening. I had come to know Anne through her business manager, who was a good friend of Leafs teammate Norm Ullman. We are pretty close to being of the same vintage, and she has always been a big Leafs fan.

One of the items produced for the closing was a list of all-time scoring at the Gardens. Here are some of the notables:

MOST GOALS SCORED AT MLG BY A MAPLE LEAF

Darryl Sittler 235
Dave Keon 226
Ron Ellis 186
Frank Mahovlich 180
Rick Vaive 174
George Armstrong 173

MOST GOALS SCORED AT MLG BY A VISITING PLAYER

Gordie Howe 93
Alex Delvecchio 62
Johnny Bucyk 57
Henri Richard 53
Jean Béliveau 51
Bobby Hull 49

MOST POINTS RECORDED AT MLG BY A MAPLE LEAF

Darryl Sittler 524
Dave Keon 521
George Armstrong 412
Borje Salming 398
Frank Mahovlich 376
Ron Ellis 360

MOST POINTS RECORDED AT MLG BY A VISITING PLAYER

Gordie Howe 126
Johnny Bucyk 87
Alex Delvecchio 80
Bobby Hull 80
Wayne Gretzky 77
Jean Béliveau 75

◄ **Anne Murray performs at the closing of Maple Leaf Gardens.**

VISITING WITH THE ARMED FORCES

The Canadian Armed Forces are made up of very special people. Not only do these brave men and women help defend our country, they also help others around the world. The Maple Leafs have a wonderful tradition of honouring a different member of the Forces at each home game – recognition they richly deserve.

On Thanksgiving weekend in 2014, I visited our Canadian Forces base in Kuwait and played ball hockey with the troops. It may seem like a small thing, but a good game of ball hockey allows those serving to take their minds off of what they go through over there, just for a little while. More than one person told me that I was their dad's hockey hero, which was nice to hear. After the stop in Kuwait, our group – which included Brian Burke, Tom Anselmi, Tim Hicks, Alan Frew, Tiger Williams, and Arlene Dickinson – went over to the Persian Gulf to visit with our forces on a warship station there. A few other members of the NHL Alumni were also with us.

The alumni also play a game on ice at the ACC on Armed Forces Night, which the Maple Leafs have hosted during a regular-season home game for a number of years now. The game is closed to the public, but it's nice for former players like me to inspire the troops and give them a little relief. Tiger has been overseas quite a number of times and has visited the Canadian base in Afghanistan. On more than one occasion, he and his group had to take cover because of an incoming missile. Even though you know there is a war going on, such events are a grim reminder that the situation can change instantly.

◀ At the Air Canada Centre in Toronto during Canadian Armed Forces Night (top);
With Tiger and Lanny on Canadian Armed Forces Night (bottom).

MY LEAFS SWEATER

In September of 1998, Mike Leonetti – my co-author on this book – released a children's book called *My Leafs Sweater*. The story features a young kid named Michael whose birthday wish is a Maple Leafs sweater with number 27 on the back, in honour of his hockey hero. He doesn't get that wish, but Mike does end up at Maple Leaf Gardens on February 7, 1976, which just happens to be the night I recorded 10 points against the Boston Bruins.

Since the book came out, many kids too young to have ever seen me play tell me I am their favourite player because of *My Leafs Sweater*. It was pretty cool to have a children's book written about me, and I have autographed many copies over the years. One father even had me sign it for his newborn son. The same kid came up to me years later and had me sign it again for his dad's 50th birthday!

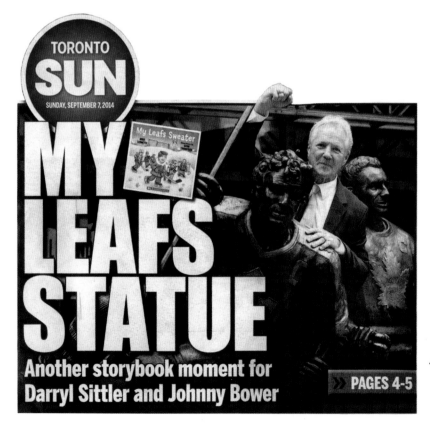

◀ *My Leafs Sweater* makes the front page.
My Leafs Sweater, featuring an illustration of me. ▶

THE DARRYL SITTLER SONG

When I turned 60, a family friend gave me a truly unique gift. Bill Swinimer (who was CEO of a company I did some work for) suggested to his singer/songwriter son Dan that he write a song in honour of the milestone. I had been Dan's favourite hockey player when he was a kid, so he was pleased to do it. Over a very short period of time, Dan and his good friend Jeff Johnson put together "The Darryl Sittler Song." Dan did the singing while Jeff played the drums and the acoustic guitar. They found other performers to play additional instruments, and brought in people who were familiar with music engineering and production. The song debuted on AM640 Radio in Toronto when Bill Watters was hosting a lunchtime show and while the station was broadcasting on location at Wayne Gretzky's restaurant in the downtown area. It was not something I was expecting at all. My family was at home with me (including my grandson Luke, who came up for a surprise visit) and we were able to listen to it together.

Dan's lyrics include so many events and people who affected my life, and the music has a Stompin' Tom Connors sort of sound to it. (You can find it on YouTube.) I think it came out pretty great!

THE DARRYL SITTLER SONG

V1
We love our Darryl Sittler
yeah he's a hockey man
my memory is foggy
how long has it been?
Ya know he's turning 60
there's nothing wrong with that
hell you can live through anything
if you've lived through Punch Imlach

V2
Remember 27 had 10 points in a game
that record goes unbroken in the Hockey Hall Of Fame
he's the first Leaf to 100 points
damn that Sit could score!
no other Leaf would match him
till the shifty Doug Gilmour

Chorus
Number 27
we miss you on the ice
your agent says you're golfing
with a 60 year old slice
Happy birthday Sittler
you really did us proud
but tell me Darryl Sittler
what are ya doin now?

V3
5 goals in a playoff game
knocked the broadstreet bullies down
we should have won that series
against them Philly clowns
60 years and counting
his legacy's alive
but his curly hair ain't seen the ice since 1985

V4
what was Ballard thinking
when he shipped Sitt to the Flyers
Clarke promised the captaincy
I guess he was a liar
tell Bobby Clarke it's over
you can't do him any harm
they put him out to pasture
like an old horse on the farm

Chorus 2

Number 27
we miss you on the ice
mouthing off to Philly
while Tiger paid the Price
Happy birthday Sittler
you really did us proud
we miss you Darryl Sittler
what are ya doin now?

Ballard made a mess of things but Sittler braved the storm
but when they traded Lanny
that's when the C was torn
a feud ensued it wasn't right but all is well today
his jersey's hangin proudly from the rafters on display

Chorus 3
Well Number 27
we miss you on the ice
you should have had Lord Stanley
But the Canada Cup was nice
Happy birthday Darryl Sittler
you really did us proud
today you're turning 60
what are ya doin now?

Number 27
we miss you on the ice
you'll always be a Maple Leaf
tho your red hair now is white
Happy birthday Darryl
you really did us proud
today you're turning 60
we hope your doin well!

The Darryl Sittler Song
Written by Dan Swinimer (Manicdown Productions) and Jeff Johnson
(Bailey Way Entertainment)
copyright © 2010
Engineered by Jeff Dawson (Jeff Dawson Productions), Kris Siegers
(Crying Light Productions) and Dan Swinimer (Manicdown
Productions)
Mixed by Jeff Dawson

CD Artwork - Kevin Fulton (Kevin Fulton Designs)
Musicians;
Drums, Bass, Acoustic Guitar, Vocals - Dan Swinimer (Jet Black Stare)
Lead Guitar - Matt Rose (The Matinee)
Banjo - Chris "Dunner" Duncombe (Run GMC)

Very Special Thanks to Bill Swinimer, and all the talented musicians,
engineers and designers that volunteered their time to make this
happen.

EIGHT

MY FAMILY

WENDY

Wendy and I were married for thirty years, and we had been together since we were teenagers. She was the most influential person in my life and in the lives of our three children. Her smile was warm and beautiful and she gave all of us great love, support, and understanding. Wendy was very dedicated to being the best wife and mother she could possibly be and she will always be remembered that way. We all led busy lives, as we were a very active group, but there was no doubt she was the backbone of our family. She was always there when we needed her most. Wendy had a great sense of humour but also had a gentle sensitivity that everyone could see and appreciate – especially me.

Wendy was also a person of great strength. Amid the on-ice chaos after I scored the overtime goal to win the 1976 Canada Cup, Alan Eagleson, the tournament organizer and my agent at the time, said, "Let me hold on to your stick." At the time, I thought it was a good idea – there were so many people on the Montreal Forum ice at that moment, and I wanted to keep the stick safe. Alan, however, just kept it. Every time I asked for the stick he refused to give it back. While this certainly bothered me, I hadn't gotten around to doing anything about it. Wendy, though, took matters into her own hands. Just before my 30th birthday, she called Eagleson and said she was coming by to pick it up so I could have it the next day as a present. He said he was leaving town. She said she would come before he left. Wendy arrived in time and I finally got my stick back, along with a poem she'd written for my birthday. If Wendy hadn't been so persistent, I don't think I'd ever have gotten that stick back!

Ten years later, when I turned 40, Wendy arranged to have me parachute out of an airplane. At first I thought she was joking, but she was serious. My good friend Dave Baker and I spent some time in the morning getting instructions, and by early afternoon we were in a small plane, 3,000 feet up in the air. I had once mentioned to Wendy that I would like to do this at some point in my life, and she remembered my words for this milestone birthday. It was an experience I will never forget! After the jump, we went home and had a great party, with many of my former teammates in attendance.

THE COTTAGE

Our family cottage in Orillia, Ontario, has been a big part of my life since I purchased it in 1978. My kids were young when we first got the place, and we spent many great summers there. It has been the site of numerous memorable parties and gatherings, including the weddings of both of my daughters. The cottage once belonged to former teammate Mike Walton, whom I first knew from the Orr-Walton Sports Camp, which ran in Orillia every summer for a number of years. By 1978, I was in position to buy a cottage, and when Mike decided to sell it, he was pleased that it went to someone he knew. The cottage has been a central place for my family from the time we first bought it and that is still the case today. We have had many happy events there, with more to come in the future.

RYAN SITTLER

My son, Ryan, was born in 1974. He was eight years old when I was traded to Philadelphia, which meant he played his minor hockey in the United States. He learned to skate in Canada and would sometimes come with me to practice or pre-game skates when I was with the Maple Leafs. However, Wendy and I tried not to expose him to the pressures of being my son when it came to playing hockey. Ryan developed into a good player and was often asked to attend summer development camps. It was a little easier for him playing south of the border.

After we settled in East Amherst, he enrolled in Nichols School, which had one of the top high-school hockey programs in western New York. Ryan was 17 when he was selected to represent the United States at the World U18 tournament in Japan. He'd also thinned out by this time, turning into a six foot two, 180-pound athlete – hockey scouts started to take notice. He could have played junior hockey but instead chose to go the college route at the University of Michigan, where he was coached by former NHL player Red Berenson. He was doing pretty well (51 points in 61 games over two seasons), and the Philadelphia Flyers took him seventh overall in the 1992 NHL Entry Draft. Ryan's selection made us the first father-son tandem to be chosen in the first round.

Ryan played in the World Junior Tournament three times and won a bronze medal with the American team in 1992. Unfortunately, a series of injuries started to hold Ryan back, and a suckerpunch during a fight in an American Hockey League game did some major facial damage. He had trouble recovering from his injuries and, in the end, couldn't stay healthy enough to develop his game – although he did manage a season in which he played in 66 contests for the AHL's Baltimore Bandits. Eventually, however, he had to retire from hockey at the age of 25. In 2012, he had to deal with the death of his wife, Cristy. He lives in Florida now with his son, Luke (who was born on September 15, 2004 – the 28th anniversary of my winning goal at the Canada Cup), and is a stepfather to two daughters – Morgan and Olivia. I am very close to Luke, and have a place in Jupiter, Florida, where I can stay while visiting Ryan and his family.

◀ Clockwise: Ryan, fishing; his son, Luke;
Ryan fishing with me and my dad, Ken.

MEAGHAN SITTLER

My daughter Meaghan was born in March 1976. The way she grew up to love the game of hockey reminded me of how I was when I was a kid. (When she turned one on March 12, 1977, I scored my 200th career goal in a 6–0 win over the Detroit Red Wings.) She played against boys, and though it sometimes got too rough out on the ice for my liking, she was a good player, so that made it a little easier for me to watch. As she got older, though, there were some tough moments. Some guys went too far, and Meaghan was definitely a target with the Sittler name on the back of her sweater. I was much happier when she started playing against girls only. Her time playing hockey was, on the whole, a wonderful experience.

Meaghan was a AAA player before attending Nichols School in Buffalo. In 1994, she enrolled at Maine's Colby College, where she became one of the top female NCAA hockey players in the United States. One year, she led the nation with 41 goals and 41 assists in 21 games. Even though her team was defeated in the first round of the NCAA tournament, she recorded eight hat tricks in her final 13 games of the season. Meaghan is the first player to have her sweater number (16) retired by Colby College.

In 1996, Meaghan represented the United States on the women's national team, bringing home a silver medal from the Pacific Rim Championship. In 1998 and 1999, she participated in the Three Nations Cup and was on the US Select team in 1999 and 2000. Meaghan also played for the Brampton Thunder of the National Women's Hockey League, one of the best teams in that league. She trained year round and really loved the game.

Meaghan is married to Amy Apps, the granddaughter of Maple Leafs legend Syl Apps and daughter of Syl Apps Jr., whom I played against in the NHL. Their son is named Sawyer Apps-Sittler. Meaghan earned a bachelor of arts in sociology and then a master's degree in social work; as of 2010, she is working as a life coach. Her background as a former elite athlete will be very helpful to her in this role.

"HER LOVE OF HOCKEY IS SOMETHING THAT CAN'T BE TAUGHT. WANTING TO IMPROVE AND BE AN ELITE PLAYER IS SOMETHING MEAGHAN HAS ALWAYS WANTED FOR HERSELF."

Darryl Sittler on daughter Meaghan's hockey career

Wedding at our cottage.

Representing the U.S. National Team.

ASHLEY SITTLER

Ashley was born in June 1981. The ambulance went to the wrong house, and so her birth took place at home. She is the spitting image of her mother, with a beautiful smile, warm heart, and infectious personality. She is married to Mike Uronick, and on July 30, 2015, they welcomed my third grandchild, Freddy, into the world. He was given the name Freddy in honour of Wendy's father.

Growing up, Ashley played hockey in Buffalo, and then went on to play at the University of Guelph. When Wendy was sick, she decided to stop playing. Ashley went back to school and graduated from Ryerson University. She currently works for Molson Coors Canada as a manager in sponsorship and events.

◀ Ashley, Wendy, and Meaghan
(left); Freddy (right).
With husband, Mike, son, Freddy,
and Lanny and Ardell McDonald.
(right); Wedding day (left). ▶

SYL APPS JR.

Syl Apps Jr. was a very good player for the Pittsburgh Penguins during the 1970s. He played alongside Jean Pronovost and Lowell MacDonald on one of the most highly skilled lines in the NHL. They scored a lot of goals and racked up a high number of points. Syl recorded 606 career points in 727 NHL games between 1970 and 1980. Syl wore number 26 for the Penguins, and when we were together for the birth of our grandchild (our daughters Meaghan and Amy are married), it was getting late on the night of February 26, 2014. We wondered if the birthdate would be the 26th (his sweater number) or if it would go to the 27th (my sweater number). Meaghan gave birth to a boy – Sawyer Apps-Sittler – a couple of hours after midnight, so number 27 was the winner on this night!

◀ Sawyer Apps-Sittler's first birthday, with his grandfathers (top);
Meaghan, Sawyer, and Amy (bottom).

LUBA

When Wendy died in 2001, I was not interested in dating anyone. I needed some time to grieve with my family. A little while later, I was doing some work for Bell Canada and attended an event for them at the Air Canada Centre. The clients in the suite that evening were the responsibility of a young lady named Luba, who also worked for Bell, although I didn't know her at the time. There was something about her that struck and stayed with me. A couple of weeks later, I followed up. I got Luba's number through the people at Bell and called to ask if she wanted me to autograph any items for her clients. I also suggested that maybe we should meet for a meal. Luba was receptive (it turned out she was single).

Luba's father and brother were big hockey fans, and when the games were on television, she had to wait until the broadcast was over before she could watch something. Luba picked up some hockey knowledge from her family's interest in the sport, but she came to know more about me through her friends, who told her about Darryl Sittler's background. We went out and had a great night together, and from that point on, things fell into place. Two and a half years later, we were married. I think this happened because I kept my heart open and was receptive to experiencing love again. I didn't want to disrespect the past – Wendy and I had been married for 30 years, and I'd been by her side throughout her battle with cancer – but life is for the living. Luba stopped the numbness I was feeling after Wendy passed away.

Luba and I have now been married for 12 years. I've found true love twice, and for that I feel very fortunate. When we reminisce about Wendy, Luba enjoys hearing the stories about how Wendy was a funny and humorous person. My circle of friends have accepted Luba, even though many were very loyal friends to Wendy too. I think this just shows what a special person Luba is, to be able to fit in and be accepted. My daughters were a little concerned at first, especially since Luba is younger than me, but with the help of counselling, we came through the challenge of blending our two families.

Our wedding day. ▶

FALON

Luba's daughter, Falon, was very young when we met. Not only was I going to be married again, I was also going to be a stepfather. I try to be a positive influence on Falon as she pursues her dreams.

Falon loves spending time with her family – she adores her nephews. She is a natural with children and my grandsons can't wait for Auntie Falon's visits.

Falon also has a great love of animals. She surprises us from time to time by bringing strays home.

When Falon isn't spending time with her family and friends, she enjoys following the latest makeup and fashion trends. She has grown up to be a beautiful young lady with a giving heart.

◀ **Falon with nephew Sawyer, on the 40th anniversary of my 10-point night.**

GARY

My brother Gary was less than two years younger than me and he also loved to play hockey. He was not a big guy (5 foot 9 nine inches and 185 pounds) but he was very determined to protect his teammates on the ice. He was a tough defenceman, twice recording over 300 penalty minutes in a season as a pro. He played junior hockey with the London Knights before starting a minor-pro career that lasted from 1972 until 1978. He played in five career games for the WHA Michigan Stags/ Baltimore Blades in 1974–75, recording one goal and one assist with 14 penalty minutes. In 1976–77, Gary won two championships – one with the Syracuse Blazers of the North American Hockey League (recording 11 points in 9 playoff games) and one with the Saginaw Gears of the International Hockey League (recording 17 points in 12 playoff games).

We played on the London Knights together for one season and if we were not playing hockey we were playing softball or fishing. We had some great times going fishing up north, and when Gary stopped playing minor pro hockey, he and his wife, Sandy, moved to Wawa, Ontario, with their two children, Jeremy and Krista.

Gary held a few different jobs (including police officer and restaurant owner) in Wawa where he lived for more than twenty-five years before a job opportunity took him to Nelson, British Columbia, in 1999. He worked in the forest industry and then in the maintenance department for a local school district and became a proud grandfather to Kohen and Ava. He continued to enjoy the northern lifestyle, which allowed him to hunt and fish as he had always done. He was very passionate about the outdoors and also became friends with many of the First Nations people who lived in the area.

Gary could be a bit of a prankster as a way of testing someone – especially newcomers. But he was really a very kind-hearted person under a somewhat rough exterior. He became a storyteller later in life, and he still loved his fish fry dinners. He suffered a heart attack on February 24, 2015, and passed away at the age of sixty-two.

My siblings and me at my mother's 80th birthday. Back row, left to right: Ken, me, Gary, Tim, Rod, Jeff, and front row: Debbie, Doris, Linda (top); From left to right: Sandy, Jeremy, Deidre, and Gary – with Kohen (bottom). ▶

GIVING BACK

Throughout my career, it has been important to me to help others. Here are some of the organizations I am proud to be involved with, and which mean a lot to me personally:

HELPING START RONALD MCDONALD HOUSE

In the late 1970s, I was visiting with an 11-year-old boy who was dying at the Hospital for Sick Children in Toronto. As I left his room after our talk, which I hope gave him some comfort, I saw his mother down the corridor, looking out the window. I went over to speak to her and learned that the family was from Sudbury, Ontario. They had been in Toronto for about 15 weeks to be with their son. The bills were piling up and the family was contemplating taking out a second mortgage on their farm. It was obviously a bad situation, but there wasn't much they could do about it; there was no place to stay in the city except for a hotel.

Just a few weeks later I got a phone call asking if I would be interested in serving as a spokesperson for a new Canadian venture to be known as Ronald McDonald House. McDonald's Restaurants of Canada was sponsoring the idea. They set a goal of $1 million to start this house for families in need – to create a "home away from home" for seriously ill children and their families. The timing could not have been better. I did lots of media for this project and, through a great amount of teamwork, we pulled it off. The first such house opened in 1981.

Fast forward to 2016. I was speaking at a hockey banquet in Melville, Saskatchewan. Following my talk, a gentleman contacted me to tell me about a young man who has the same type of bone cancer that Terry Fox did. I visited Chad in hospital in Toronto. He had had his leg amputated up to his pelvis. When I asked if he wanted to take a picture I tried to lean down a little but Chad insisted on trying to stand up as much as he could by using the bars above his bed to pull himself up. I told him he could be an inspiration to other people just like Terry Fox was for so many people. Chad is certainly an inspiration to me. Chad's dad, Dallas, told me how much it meant to their family to be able to stay at Ronald McDonald House. All that work to get that first house going was all worth it. There are 14 houses across Canada today.

A NEW INITIATIVE FOR DOWN'S SYNDROME

My nephew Jeremy (son of my late brother, Gary) has a son, Kohen, with Down's syndrome. Inspired by Kohen, I have joined forces with a Toronto company called LocoMobi. Under the leadership of CEO Grant Furlane, LocoMobi is working on a pilot project to build independent housing for adults with Down's in the Greater Toronto Area, and to create work opportunities. We want adults with Down's to know they can contribute to society in a meaningful way while also maintaining some independence.

Our first walk/run in 2015 was a great success – we had over 1,200 participants and raised over $100,000. The event is known as the Go21 – Halton Walk for Down Syndrome. "Go" stands for the advancement and growth of the Down's syndrome community, while "21" represents the tripling of the 21st chromosome that determines Down diagnosis. In July 2016, Have a Heart for Down Syndrome is hosting Sink One for Jake, a golf tournament named for Jake Hardy, one of the inspirations for the HHDS. I'm excited to see where this initiative goes.

Team LocoMobi.
Back row, fourth from right: Grant Furlane.
Fifth from right: Jake Hardy. ▲

SCOTIABANK HOCKEY COLLEGE

In the 1970s, hockey broadcaster and writer Brian McFarlane approached the Bank of Nova Scotia with an idea. Brian thought using hockey would be a great way to get kids interested in banking and saving, and he suggested starting the Scotiabank Hockey College. By opening a savings account, each child would get an account book and would automatically be enrolled in the Scotiabank Hockey College. As part of their enrolment, each youngster would receive a newsletter, *The Hockey College News*, featuring hockey stories and photos, as well as articles and tips on how to manage money. When the bank decided to give the college a higher profile, they recruited Jean Béliveau and Gordie Howe as ambassadors (both were retired at the time) and filmed some television commercials. The program was a great success.

In 1979, the bank wanted to bring on another player and asked if I would be interested. I said I would be happy to join, and "Darryl's Diary" soon became a regular newsletter feature. I was introduced as a regular contributor on the cover of the September 1979 issue. I was called the first official "captain" of the college. I wrote: "I have followed the progress of the Hockey College with great interest and I'm pleased to lend my support to a program that assists young players in developing basic hockey skills while encouraging sportsmanship, fitness, education and citizenship."

I strongly believed that those were vital things for all hockey-playing kids to learn. It was a great experience. Joining the college was another case of life coming full circle: the very first bank account I opened in St. Jacobs was with the Bank of Nova Scotia!

September 1979 cover of *Hockey College News*. ▶

Volume 8, Issue 12
September 1979

SCOTIABANK HOCKEY COLLEGE
News

Sittler signs with Hockey College

PLUS
Denis Potvin, defenseman of the year
Fred Shero, the coach nobody knows
Rookie award goes to Smith
Plus much more

WENDY BEARS

My wife, Wendy, was afflicted with colon cancer (the number-two killer of all cancers), and it would eventually take her life, despite her brave efforts to fight the disease. Mariellen Black was going through the same battle when she heard about Wendy's situation. She contacted us and asked if we would be willing to help raise awareness of this type of cancer. Wendy, who normally shunned the public spotlight, said she would be there to help out. At a news conference to announce an initiative to promote colorectal screening (today Screen Colons Canada, www.screencolons.ca), Wendy said that if her experience could help save even one life, it would be worth it.

After Wendy was diagnosed, Bunnie Schwartz, of Colon Cancer Canada, also contacted us, after their annual walk/run. Bunnie's husband, Howard, was going through the same treatment as Wendy at the time. Bunnie's sister, Maureen, had died of colon cancer in 1996, and with Maureen's daughter, Amy Lerman-Elmaleh, she had co-founded Colon Cancer Canada (www.coloncancer.ca).

My daughter Meaghan moved back home so she could be with Wendy for the last year of her life. When Wendy was in the final stages, Meaghan called me. Wendy was in a hospice at the time, where she was being well cared for, but Meaghan suggested that Wendy really wanted to go home. At first the hospice was reluctant to let Wendy go, but we quickly made the necessary arrangements and Wendy was home within two hours. She died 24 hours later. We were so grateful that it happened at home. It was a peaceful ending and she was surrounded by family.

Our friends at Colon Cancer Canada asked if they could name their new program after Wendy, and so the "Wendy Bears" program, to help people who wanted to die at home but did not have the financial means to make it happen, began. The sale of the stuffed bears helps to raise money for people in this situation. Wendy Bears have helped many to spend their final few days at home as is their wish. They have become an inspiration to many.

SCOTIABANK BAYCREST PRO-AM

For a few years now, I have been a regular participant in the Scotiabank Baycrest Pro-Am in support of Alzheimer's. The tournament sees hockey fans lace up their skates to face off against some of the game's greatest. In the past, we've had former NHL players such as Mike Modano, Adam Oates, Larry Murphy, Mike Gartner, Wendel Clark, Curtis Joseph, and Darcy Tucker in for the tournament, which has very close ties to the NHL Alumni Association. The money raised goes to the Baycrest Foundation, which encourages research, education, and care in the battle against Alzheimer's and other dementia-related diseases. The Baycrest Foundation has also received great support from Gordie Howe and his family. Gordie's wife, Colleen, died from a form of dementia and he wanted to help others facing the same situation. In the 10 years since it started, this two-day event has raised over $25 million.

I got involved after meeting Joey Arfin, when he won dinner and drinks with me at a charity auction. I was Joey's childhood hockey hero and we hit it off right away, establishing a strong personal relationship. Each year, the teams are drafted according to who has raised the most money, but Joey, who plays forward and wears number 66, always has me on his team – he will not trade me away!

Joey has been part of the tournament since the beginning. His grandmother died from complications from Alzheimer's and his grandfather succumbed to Parkinson's disease. "This is much more than a hockey tournament for me," Joey says. "I know the importance of the funds raised through this event, which will support others coping with this awful disease. I am truly honoured to be part of the Pro-Am community and play alongside NHL greats with this shared vision in mind."

Anyone interested in playing or raising funds for the Baycrest Foundation can visit www.scotiabankproam.com.

With Joey Arfin. ▶

SUN LIFE FINANCIAL AND DIABETES

My family has been greatly affected by diabetes. At age 59, my grandmother lost her sight as a result of the disease. She died at 66 of complications related to diabetes. My father was diagnosed with type 2 in his late 40s and suffered a series of small strokes. He died of a heart attack when he was 62. Two of my brothers, Gary and Ken, were also diagnosed with type 2. Gary suffered a fatal heart attack in February 2015 at the age of 62.

When Sun Life Financial approached me about working with them on their diabetes campaign, I was pleased to help. Since 2011, the company has contributed $13 million to raise awareness of and fight diabetes and its related complications. I think they made a great choice when they decided to commit their philanthropic dollars to this important cause. So many people in Canada and around the world are affected.

Knowing my family history has made me very proactive when it comes to my health, and I found out recently that I have prediabetes (indicated by a rise in glucose levels). I work with doctors on a regular basis to help with prevention, and I try to exercise as part of a healthier approach to living. I'm also very realistic. I know that there will be moments where I want to satisfy my persistent sweet tooth!

To find out more about Sun Life's campaign, go to https://www.sunlife.ca/ca/About+us/Donations+and+sponsorships/Supporting+health/Team+up+against+diabetes?vgnLocale=en_CA&sf=true.

THE SPECIAL OLYMPICS

Throughout my playing career and up until today, I have always been proud to be involved with Special Olympics – which supports more than 40,000 Canadians with intellectual disabilities who take part in its programs. The Limitless gala celebrated the joy, determination, and great potential of Special Olympics athletes. That night, more than 750 people got to meet an amazing group of celebrities and athletes. Jamie Salé, Bob McKenzie, Elaine Lui, Curt Harnett, Darren Dreger, David Pelletier, Mark Tewksbury, Rick Mercer, and 2016 Olympic medal contenders Damian Warner, Melissa Bishop, and Shawnacy Barber came out for the event, as did many Special Olympics athletes.

PRINCESS MARGARET HOSPITAL
ROAD HOCKEY TO CONQUER CANCER

Another great cause I am involved with is the Princess Margaret Road Hockey to Conquer Cancer tournament. This all-day event features a hundred teams battling it out to raise funds for personalized cancer medicine at the Princess Margaret Cancer Centre, one of the top five cancer research centres in the world. The top fundraising teams get to select their favourite hockey legend or celebrity via a draft. The spirited but friendly competition has been going on for five years now.

The 2015 event had a good showing of former Maple Leafs, including Johnny Bower, Bobby Baun, Ron Ellis, Paul Henderson, Glenn Anderson, and Eric Lindros, among others. There were over 1,400 participants and 141 teams and an impressive $2.4 million was raised during the one-day extravaganza.

Special Olympics athlete Emily Boycott.

Road Hockey to Conquer Cancer 2015. I look forward to this event every year.

EASTER SEALS AND MARCH OF DIMES

One of the things I remember from my childhood was a calendar that Maple Leafs Gardens would put out each year, featuring a Toronto player and a child in need. As captain of the Maple Leafs, you are a spokesperson for the team, and you take it upon yourself to do what players such as Ted Kennedy, Tim Horton, and Frank Mahovlich did for young people years ago. Two of the programs the organization gave great support to when I was captain were the Ontario March of Dimes and Easter Seals.

Easter Seals began in 1922 and more than 90 years later still provides support for children and youth with physical disabilities. The March of Dimes started as a fundraising organization. Mothers would go door to door looking for a donation – of just one dime – for research to find a cure for polio. Since the 1960s the organization has served the needs of those with a range of physical disabilities.

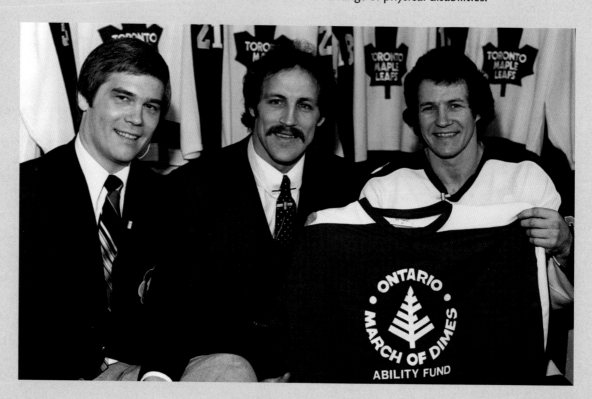

With Dave Hodge and Tony Gabriel in the early 1970s. ▲

MCMASTER CHILDREN'S HOSPITAL ROOFTOP PLAYGROUNDS

Recently, I was happy to be involved in the creation of rooftop playgrounds at McMaster Children's Hospital in Hamilton, Ontario. The three play spaces opened in 2015 after five years of planning. It was really a great feeling to visit the new playgrounds and see children and teenagers benefiting from the new spaces and enjoying themselves.

The idea was made possible through generous donations from a variety of groups. Rob Baboth, a director and vice-president at Foresters Life Insurance Company, got me interested in this project and he started out by donating the proceeds from the Dianne Baboth Memorial Tournament, a golf tournament held in memory of his mother. The Hamilton Health Sciences Foundation partnered with the tournament, and a few years later the rest is history. In June of 2015 the three sites were named the Dianne Baboth Memorial Playgrounds.

▲ Mary Beth, Arden, Dylan, and Rob Baboth.

GOOD MEMORIES: first row, L to R: With Daniela and Rob Fiocca, on the set of the *Late Show with David Letterman*; Sharon and Dave Dougherty, Anne and Art Frank; Ardell McDonald and Wendy; second row, L to R: (back row) Luba, me, Ardell McDonald, Brenda Williams, Tiger Williams, Tammy Cail, Jim Peters, (front row) Lanny McDonald, Carol Dionne, Marcel Dionne, Risto Laamanen, Marlene Boland; Tim, Norma-Jean, Lindsay, and Lauren; Tom and Marg Hussey; third row, L to R: Pauline and Ray Perepelycia; Ryan, Fred Bibbings, Wendy, me, Eve Bibbings, Meaghan, Diane Sauchuk, Ashley, and Pooghan!; Colleen Burns and Wendy; fourth row, L to R: Ange Valenti; Me and Luba, Lexy and David Courtney; Naddy and Bill Watters and Graeme Clark.

Continued: first row, L to R: Dave Heffler and me; Phil Davidson and Debbie Fernandes, Luba and me; Joe and Eva;
second row, L to R: me, Wendy, Ashley, Meaghan, Ryan, Zane Cohen, Bunnie Schwartz; me, Tom Hussey, Bill Swinimer, Dan Swinimer, Tim Hicks; Morgan, Cristy,
Olivia, and Luke, with Ryan; third row, L to R: Mark and Dianne Hawkins with Michael Burgess; Betty and Mel Stevens; Dave and Joan Baker;
fourth row, L to R: Elizabeth Daponte and Walter Henry; Louis and Marla Reznick and me; my grandsons, Luke, Freddy, and Sawyer.

DARRYL TODAY: Q & A

Q: Since your return to the Maple Leafs you have played a big role in the Maple Leafs alumni group. How do you like the way the alumni are treated today?

A: Before Cliff Fletcher there really was no formal alumni association, and then he and Steve Stavro (late owner of the team) put one together. I think we have one of the best alumni groups now. Our members are out at many functions over the course of a year. We had a great turnout for the Winter Classic in 2014 in Detroit and we were able to ice two teams of alumni members. In December 2016, Leafs and Red Wings alumni will meet again to play an outdoor game at BMO Field, in Toronto, to celebrate the 100th anniversary of the Toronto Maple Leafs franchise.

Q: Cliff Fletcher also offered you the chance to coach the team at one point but you turned the opportunity down. Why was that?

A: I was offered the interim coaching job after Pat Burns was let go and it was very flattering. I did consider it but I had no coaching experience and felt that was not going to be fair to the players. I was never passionate about coaching and was not prepared to deal with the other aspects of the job, like dealing with the media on a daily basis. It might have been different if I aspired to get into coaching but that was not the case for me.

Q: You had the chance to work under the leadership of Richard Peddie when he was in charge of running the business at Maple Leaf Sports and Entertainment. What was that like from where you sat?

A: Richard Peddie was someone I liked because he was very approachable. He built a successful organization to the point where Bell and Rogers paid top dollar to buy MLSE. Many of the very successful ventures like Maple Leaf Square and Real Sports were Richard's vision. I reported to Tom Anselmi, who had been with MLSE since the late 1990s (helping to develop the Air Canada Centre) in a few different roles. Tom was very instrumental in developing the Maple Leafs alumni association and in honouring our troops serving overseas. He helped to organize many trips to visit the men and women serving in Afghanistan. I went on one of those trips and it was an experience I will always remember.

Q: The media has changed so much from the days when you were captain of the team. Is the constant scrutiny too difficult for Maple Leaf players to handle?

A: The power of the regular media and social media (which did not exist when I played) is much stronger than ever before. Beat guys used to be on our plane as we travelled, so we were all used to each other and certain lines were never crossed. Today there is a need for interviews and press conferences to be more structured. Players never understand what it is like to be a Maple Leaf until they get here. It's different in Toronto and Montreal for you and for your family. Some players have the personality to handle the expectations and they understand they have to respond even though there are no formal rules about having to deal with media. I think a very talented player like Phil Kessel did not always want to deal with the media and as a result they were hard on him. It is expected that a star player will respond when he is questioned. In my day, there was a higher level of respect between players and the people who covered the team.

Q: What do you like about hockey today? What would you like to see change?

A: The best thing about hockey today is that we have so many young, highly skilled players entering the game year after year. There are more high quality young players in hockey than ever before, with more on the way.

I don't like the cycling in the corners of the rinks. It reduces the quality scoring chances and keeps the shots-on-net total too low. I also think that at times there are too many penalties called – almost like there are too many fouls called in basketball. It has reached the point where players will turn their bodies the wrong way or dive like in soccer just to draw a penalty call. We get more power plays this way but this mindset is different than when I played in the NHL. I don't think I would like to see the nets get bigger because that would be too radical a change.

Q: Can you tell us about the house where you grew up?

A: The house I grew up in in St. Jacobs was actually purchased by a business that is right across the street from it and they use it as an administrative office. They put up a new plaque in my honour after I was named to the Maple Leafs Legends Row, so that will hopefully be there for a long time. If you look out from the front of that house you can see the tombstones of both my grandfather and father, who are buried at the cemetery close by. The street has been renamed Darryl Sittler Court.

FOR THE RECORD

POSITION: **C**   SHOOTS: **Left**
HEIGHT: **6'0" (183 cm)**
WEIGHT: **190 lbs. (86 kg)**

BORN: **September 18, 1950, in Kitchener, Ontario**
DRAFT: **Toronto, 1st round (8th overall), 1970 NHL Amateur**

NHL

Season	Team	Lge	GP	G	A	Pts	PIM	GP	G	A	Pts	PIM
					REGULAR SEASON					PLAYOFFS		
1970–71	Toronto Maple Leafs	NHL	49	10	8	18	37	6	2	1	3	31
1971–72	Toronto Maple Leafs	NHL	74	15	17	32	44	3	0	0	0	2
1972–73	Toronto Maple Leafs	NHL	78	29	48	77	69	—	—	—	—	—
1973–74	Toronto Maple Leafs	NHL	78	38	46	84	55	4	2	1	3	6
1974–75	Toronto Maple Leafs	NHL	72	36	44	80	47	7	2	1	3	15
1975–76	Toronto Maple Leafs	NHL	79	41	59	100	90	10	5	7	12	19
1976–77	Toronto Maple Leafs	NHL	73	38	52	90	89	9	5	16	21	4
1977–78	Toronto Maple Leafs	NHL	80	45	72	117	100	13	3	8	11	12
1978–79	Toronto Maple Leafs	NHL	70	36	51	87	69	6	5	4	9	17
1979–80	Toronto Maple Leafs	NHL	73	40	57	97	62	3	1	2	3	10
1980–81	Toronto Maple Leafs	NHL	80	43	53	96	77	3	0	0	0	4
1981–82	Toronto Maple Leafs	NHL	38	18	20	38	24	—	—	—	—	—
1981–82	Philadelphia Flyers	NHL	35	14	18	32	50	4	3	1	4	6

Season	Team	Lge	GP	G	A	Pts	PIM	GP	G	A	Pts	PIM
1982–83	Philadelphia Flyers	NHL	80	43	40	83	60	3	1	0	1	4
1983–84	Philadelphia Flyers	NHL	76	27	36	63	38	3	0	2	2	7
1984–85	Detroit Red Wings	NHL	61	11	16	27	37	2	0	2	2	0
	NHL Totals		**1096**	**484**	**637**	**1121**	**948**	**76**	**29**	**45**	**74**	**13**

OTHER

———— REGULAR SEASON ————   ———— PLAYOFFS ————

Season	Team	Lge	GP	G	A	Pts	PIM	GP	G	A	Pts	PIM
1967–68	London Nationals	OHA-Jr.	54	22	41	63	84	5	5	2	7	6
1968–69	London Knights	OHA-Jr.	53	34	65	99	90	6	2	5	7	11
1969–70	London Knights	OHA-Jr.	54	42	48	90	126	12	4	12	16	32
1976–77	Canada	Can-Cup	7	4	2	6	4					
1978–79	NHL All-Stars	Ch-Cup	3	0	1	1	0					
1981–82	Canada	WEC-A	10	4	3	7	2					
1982–83	Canada	WEC-A	10	3	1	4	12					

TRANSACTIONS

January 20, 1982: **Traded to Philadelphia by Toronto for Rich Costello, Hartford's 2nd round choice (previously acquired, Toronto selected Peter Ihnacak) in 1982 Entry Draft, and future considerations (Ken Strong).**

October 10, 1984: **Traded to Detroit by Philadelphia for Murray Craven and Joe Paterson.**

ACKNOWLEDGEMENTS

The text for this book is based on interviews Mike Leonetti conducted directly with Darryl Sittler. In addition, two previous books (*Sittler at Centre* with Brian McFarlane and *Sittler* with Chrys Goyens) were extensively consulted. Some material is drawn from online, television, and print interviews where Darryl Sittler was quoted directly.

The authors would like to thank: Mike Ferriman, Paul Cookson, Andrew Jackson, John Iaboni, Howard Berger, Graig Abel, Doug Ball, Brian Logie, Bruce Huff, Dennis Miles, Michelle Butnick-Press, Craig Campbell, Julia Holland, Paul Patskou, Carmen Notaro, Sean Thompson, Mike Kelly, Lisa Harmatuk, Andrea Gordon, and Jason Kaye. Mike Leonetti would like to thank his wife, Maria, and his son, David, for their help. Special thanks to everyone at Penguin Random House Canada who helped put this book together and in particular to Jenny Bradshaw, Doug Pepper, and Scott Sellers.

ILLUSTRATION CREDITS

Hockey Hall of Fame: pages i, ii, vii, 39 (right), 54, 99, 108 (bottom), 112, 122, 147 / Toronto Star: iv, xi, 3, 11 (bottom), 12, 18, 36, 41, 52 (top), 56 (bottom), 60 (top), 63, 64, 67, 68, 70, 75 (bottom), 76 (top), 95, 98, 125, 126, 129, 130 (bottom), 133 (left), 134, 137 / Getty Images: 15 (top), 52 (bottom), 91 (bottom), 100, 108 (top), 125, 145, 149, 167 / Canadian Press: 15 (bottom), 30, 91 (top), 96, 97, 134 / London Free Press: 27 (bottom) / Harold Barkley: 28, 39 (left), 56 (top), 76 (bottom), 81, 82, 130 (top) / Western Libraries: 32 / York University Archives / Toronto Telegram Collection: 44, 47, 48 (top), 55, 119 (right) / Dennis Miles: 51, 72, 78, 81, 103, 110, 111, 113, 115 (top), 116, 120, 151, 212 / Graig Abel: 87, 164 / Scholastic Books: 174, 175 / Paul Cookson (adarmygroup.com): 209 / Second City Television: 50 / Frameworth Sports Marketing: xii (Barry Gray), 43 / Robert Shaver: 85 / courtesy of the author: vii, 4, 7, 8, 11 (top), 16 (Terry Hancey), 20, 23, 24, 25, 27 (top), 35, 43 (top), 48 (bottom), 58, 59, 60 (bottom), 75 (top), 81, 88, 92, 93, 103 (left), 104, 107, 115, 119, 124, 133, 138, 141, 142, 143, 153, 154, 157, 159, 160, 163, 168, 171, 172, 176, 177, 178, 181, 182, 183, 185, 186, 187, 188, 191, 192, 195, 197, 198, 199, 200, 201, 202, 203, 204, 205, 206, 207.